All Day Brunch

All Day Brunch

SIMPLE MEALS FOR EVERY DAY

Lucia Logan

NEW
HOLLAND

Contents

 # Introduction

This book features a full range of delicious brunch dishes. With sweet and savoury recipes, there are plenty of options to choose from when having a brunch at home for yourself or for a group of people.

Many of the recipes listed in this book use the ever-versatile egg in the form of quiches, flans, frittatas, custards, soufflés, omelettes, crêpes and pancakes.

Nature designed eggs as the food source for developing chicks. Eggs, particularly chicken eggs, are also an excellent food for humans because of their high protein content, low cost and ready availability. One can correctly state, 'If there is an egg in the house, there is a meal in the house'.

Eggs are extremely versatile and are used throughout the kitchen, either served alone or as an ingredient in a prepared dish. Eggs are used to provide texture, flavour, structure, moisture and nutrition in everything from soups and sauces to breads and pastries. High quality and freshness are critical for their proper use. The primary parts of an egg are the shell, yolk and albumen. The shell composed of calcium carbonate, is the outmost covering of the egg. It prevents microbes from entering and moisture from escaping, and also protects the egg during handling and transport.

The breed of the hen determines shell colour; for chickens it can range from bright white to brown. Shell colour has no effect on quality, flavour or nutrition. The yolk is the yellow portion of the egg. It constitutes just over one third of the egg and contains three quarters of the calories, most of the minerals and vitamins and all of the fat.

The yolk also contains lecithin, the compound responsible for emulsification in products such as Hollandaise sauce and mayonnaise. Egg yolk solidifies (coagulates) at temperatures between 65°C–70°C. Although the colour of the yolk may vary depending on the hen's feed, colour does not affect quality or nutritional content. The albumen is the clear portion of the egg as is often referred to as the egg white. It constitutes about two thirds of the egg and contains more than half of the protein and riboflavin.

Egg white coagulates, becoming firm and opaque, at temperatures between 62°C–65°C. An often-misunderstood portion of the egg is the chalazae cords. These thick, twisted strands of egg anchor the yolk in place. They are neither imperfections nor embryos, the more prominent the chalazae, the fresher the egg. Chalazae do not interfere with cooking or with whipping egg whites.

Eggs are sold in jumbo, extra large, large, medium and small as determined by weight per dozen. Food service operators generally use large eggs.

When people refer to an 'egg', they generally mean a chicken egg. But other eggs are sometimes used in the kitchen. The bantam eggs are popular and come from breeds of smaller chickens; they are about half the size of chicken eggs, but have the same characteristics. A duck egg has an off-white shell and a richer flavour with a higher fat content than a chicken egg. When boiled, the duck egg turns bluish and the yolk turns red-orange. A goose egg has a white shell and is four to five times larger than a chicken egg with a richer flavour. A Guinea fowl egg has an ivory shell flecked with brown; it has a more delicate flavour than that of a chicken egg. An emu egg is twenty times as large as a chicken's egg its shell is thick and dark green. The partridge egg is a small egg with a white, buff or olive shell and a mild flavour. A quail egg is a richly flavoured egg; it is small with a speckled brown shell. The turkey egg is a large egg with a brown shell and a delicate flavour. A turtle egg is a reptile's egg with a mild, rich flavour; its soft shell is buff or speckled.

Improper handling quickly diminishes egg quality. Eggs should be stored at 4°C/40°F and at a relative humidity of 70%–80%. Eggs will age more during one day at room temperature than they will during one week under proper refrigeration.

As eggs age, the white becomes thinner and the yolk becomes flatter. Although this will change the appearance of poached or fried eggs, age has little effect on nutrition or behaviour during cooking procedures. Older eggs however, should be used for hard cooking, as the shells are easier to remove than those on fresh eggs.

Cartons of fresh, uncooked eggs will keep for at least four to five weeks beyond the pack date if properly refrigerated. Hard cooked eggs left in their shells and refrigerated should be used within one week.

Store eggs away from strongly flavoured foods to reduce odor absorption. Rotate egg stocks to maintain freshness. Do not use dirty, cracked or broken eggs as they may contain bacteria or other contaminates. Frozen eggs should be thawed in the refrigerator and used only in dishes that will be thoroughly cooked, such as baked products.

Eggs are a potentially hazardous food. Rich in protein, they are an excellent breeding ground for bacteria. Salmonella is of particular concern with eggs and egg products, because this bacterium is commonly found in a chicken's intestinal tract.

Although shells are cleaned at packing houses, some bacteria may remain. Therefore, to prevent contamination, it is best to avoid mixing a shell with the liquid egg. Inadequately cooking or improperly storing eggs may lead to food-borne illnesses.

Never leave an egg dish at room temperature for more than one hour, including preparation and service time. Never re-use a container after it has held raw eggs without thoroughly cleaning and sanitising it.

Eggs contain vitamins A, D, K and B-complex. They are rich in minerals and do not contain as much cholesterol as was once feared. In fact the American Heart Association now suggests that it is acceptable to consume up to four eggs per week as part of a balanced diet.

Basics

Porridge

¾ cup rolled oats
2 cups water
2 tablespoons brown sugar
⅓ cup milk

1 Place the oats and 1½ cups of the water in a medium bowl. Cover and soak at room temperature overnight.
2 Transfer the oats and liquid to a medium saucepan. Add the remaining water and bring to the boil. Reduce the heat and simmer, stirring, for 10 minutes or until the liquid has been absorbed. Divide the porridge between 2 serving bowls. Sprinkle with brown sugar and serve with cold milk.

serves 2

Thai porridge

½ cup large tapioca soaked in 1 cup boiling water overnight
1 cup milk (skim, full cream or rice)
1 tablespoon sugar
1 tablespoon shredded coconut

1 Place the soaked tapioca in a saucepan over high heat. Add milk, stirring constantly until it boils.
2 Reduce the heat and simmer for 20 minutes. Add the sugar and shredded coconut to the porridge. (A whisked egg can be added here for extra nutrition.)
3 Cook gently for one more minute. Serve warm with yoghurt, honey and chopped cashew nuts.

serves 2

Bircher muesli

1 cup rolled oats
1 cup apple juice
1 apple, grated
½ cup natural yoghurt

1 Place the oats and apple juice in a bowl. Cover with cling wrap and soak for 2 hours or overnight in the refrigerator.
2 Stir through the grated apple and yoghurt. Divide amongst two serving bowls.

serves 2

Date & ginger breakfast bars

½ cup wholemeal rolled rice flakes
pinch salt
2 tablespoons rice or maple syrup
1 tablespoon sugar-free apricot jam
1 teaspoon almond essence
1 cup dates, chopped
2 oz/60 g desiccated coconut
2 oz/60g shredded coconut
2 oz/60 g crystalised ginger, chopped
2 oz/60 g ground almonds
2 tablespoons rice flour
1 tablespoon psyllium

1 Line a 9 x 3 in/22 x 8 cm slice tin with baking paper. Place the rice flakes, salt and 7 oz/200 ml of cold water into a deep microwave dish. Cover and microwave on high for 3 minutes, then let stand for 3 minutes.
2 Add the rice flake mixture to other ingredients, mix well and press into the prepared tin. Bake for 20 minutes.
3 Remove from the oven and cut the mixture into four bars. Place the cut bars back into the oven on a baking tray and bake for a further 20 minutes, turning once. Let cool before wrapping.

makes 4 bars

Blueberries & yoghurt

3½ oz/100 g pecans
2 cups vanilla yoghurt
1 teaspoon ground cinnamon
3 cups blueberries

1 Preheat the oven to 350°F/180°C.
2 Spread the pecans on a baking tray and toast in the oven for 10 minutes or until lightly toasted. Coarsely chop.
3 Combine the yoghurt and cinnamon in a small bowl. Layer the yoghurt, blueberries and pecans in two glass serving bowls or cups.

serves 2

French toast

1 egg
¼ cup milk
2 slices bread

Savoury toast
salt and freshly ground black pepper

Sweet toast
1 tablespoon sugar
1 teaspoon vanilla essence
½ teaspoon ground cinnamon

1 Whisk together the egg and milk. For savoury toast, add salt and pepper to the mixture and whisk well. For sweet toast, add sugar, vanilla essence and cinnamon to the mixture and whisk well.
2 Melt a nob of butter in a frying pan. Dip the bread slices in the egg mixture, covering both sides. Place in the heated pan and cook for a few minutes, both sides over medium heat.
3 Serve with your favourite breakfast spread.

serves 1

Bacon and egg pie

2 sheets puff pastry, thawed
1 medium brown onion, finely chopped
4 oz/125 g bacon, diced
2 tablespoons spicy chutney
6 medium eggs
salt and pepper
1 tablespoon milk

1 Preheat oven to 400°F/200°C and lightly grease a 8 in/20 cm square ovenproof dish. Line the dish with 1 sheet of pastry.
2 Sprinkle onion and bacon evenly over the pastry, then dot the chutney on top. Break eggs evenly over the top, pricking the yolks so they run slightly. Season with salt and pepper. Carefully position second sheet of pastry over filling, trim edges and secure pastry by pressing down edges firmly using a fork, then brush pastry with milk.
3 Bake for 40 minutes or until risen and golden. To serve, cut into squares.
4 Serve hot or cold with grilled vine-ripened cherry tomatoes and a leafy green salad.

Note: If you prefer, you can use chopped baby spinach instead of bacon in this recipe.

serves 6

Wholewheat waffles

½ cup wholewheat pastry flour
½ cup wholewheat flour
2 egg whites
1½ tablespoons safflower oil
2 tablespoons apple sauce
2 tablespoons honey
¼ teaspoon salt
2 teaspoons baking powder
1 tablespoon soymilk

1 Mix all ingredients with ⅔ cup water until just combined.
2 Heat waffle iron. Pour in batter until almost full, close and cook for approximately 4 minutes or until golden brown.
3 Serve with fresh fruit of your choice and drizzled with maple syrup.

serves 4

Waffles with grilled banana

2 bananas, peeled and halved lengthwise
4 waffles
⅓ cup vanilla yoghurt
2 tablespoons maple syrup

1 Cook the bananas in a non-stick frying pan on medium-low heat for 2 minutes on each side or until golden brown.
2 Meanwhile, cook the waffles in a toaster until warmed and golden brown.
3 Arrange waffles on two serving plates. Place the grilled bananas on top and dollop with yoghurt. Drizzle with maple syrup and serve.

serves 2

Crumpets

4 cups unbleached flour
2 teaspoons yeast
¾ cream of tartar
2 teaspoons salt
1 teaspoon sugar
16½ oz/500 ml warm water
½ teaspoon baking soda (bicarbonate of soda)
5 oz (150 ml) warm milk

1 In a large bowl, add the flour, yeast, cream of tartar, salt and sugar and mix. Add the warm water and mix very well until a thick batter forms. Knead well by hand or spoon until the dough is thick and smooth. Cover and allow to rise for 1 hour.
2 Add the bicarbonate of soda to the warm milk and add to the dough, incorporating well so that there are no remaining lumps.
3 Grease crumpet rings and heat a cast-iron griddle, frypan or electric frypan and grease very lightly. Place the crumpet rings on the griddle and add 2 tablespoons of batter to each crumpet ring. (Test one crumpet first to check the consistency of the batter—holes should form in the surface of the dough after 3-4 minutes. If not, add a little more water to the batter, then proceed). Once the correct consistency is achieved, pour about 2 tablespoons of batter into each greased ring.
4 When the surface of bread is full of holes, remove the crumpet ring and, using a palette knife, turn the crumpet and cook the other side for a minute or two until light golden. Continue with the remaining batter.
5 Serve with butter and honey or whatever takes your fancy.

serves 4

Jewish egg loaf

3 cups unbleached bread flour
1 teaspoon salt
⅓ cup sugar
1 tablespoon yeast
2 eggs
2 tablespoons oil
1 egg, beaten
1 teaspoon poppy seeds

1 Mix flour, salt, sugar and yeast in a large mixing bowl. Add eggs, oil and ⅔ cup warm
   water and knead by hand until the dough is very soft and silky, and quite elastic. Allow
   it to rise until doubled in size.
2 Punch down dough. Divide the dough into three equal portions and roll each one into
   a rope, making sure that they are all of equal length and tapered at each end. Braid
   the three ropes into a firm plait and tuck the ends under. Allow the dough to rise on a
   greased oven tray until doubled in size.
3 When risen, brush with beaten egg and sprinkle with poppy or sesame seeds.
4 Preheat oven to 350°F/180°C. Bake for around 40 minutes then remove from the tray
   to a wire rack for cooling.

serves 8

Soda bread

1⅓ cup all-purpose (plain) flour
1 teaspoon baking soda (bicarbonate of soda)
1 teaspoon salt
1½ oz (45 g) butter
2 cups buttermilk or milk

1 Preheat oven to 400°F/200°C.
2 Sift the flour, baking soda and salt into a bowl. Rub in the butter, using your fingertips, until the mixture resembles coarse breadcrumbs. Make a well in the center of the flour mixture, pour in the milk or buttermilk and, using a round-ended knife, mix to form a soft dough.
3 Turn dough onto a floured surface and knead lightly until smooth. Shape into an 7 in/18 cm round, and place on a buttered and floured baking tray. Score dough into eighths using a sharp knife. Dust lightly with flour and bake for 35–40 minutes, or until the loaf sounds hollow when tapped on the base.

serves 8

Basil beer bread

2 cups self-rising (self-raising) flour, sifted
2 oz/60 g sugar
¾ cup fresh basil, chopped
1 teaspoon crushed black peppercorns
1 cup beer, at room temperature

1 Preheat oven to 350°F/180°C.
2 Place flour, sugar, basil, peppercorns and beer in a bowl and mix to make a soft dough.
3 Place dough in a buttered and lined 4 x 8 in/11 x 21cm loaf tin and bake for 50 minutes or until bread is cooked when tested with a skewer.
4 Stand bread in the tin for 5 minutes before turning onto a wire rack to cool. Serve warm or cold.

Note: This bread is delicious spread with olive or sun-dried tomato paste. Any beer may be used; you can experiment with light and dark ales and even stout to achieve different results.

makes one loaf

Banana and date loaf

2 cups self-rising (self-raising) flour
1 teaspoon baking soda
pinch of salt
1 teaspoon ground cinnamon
½ cup caster sugar
¾ cup fresh dates, chopped
2 eggs, lightly beaten
1 cup milk
2 ripe bananas, mashed

1 Preheat oven to 350°F/180°C and line the base and sides of a 23 x 13 cm loaf tin with baking paper.
2 Sift flour, baking soda, salt and cinnamon into a large bowl. Stir in sugar and dates.
3 Combine eggs, milk and bananas in a bowl and whisk until well combined. Stir egg mixture into dry ingredients until well combined.
4 Pour mixture into prepared loaf tin. Bake for 40–45 minutes, test with a skewer to make sure bread is cooked.
5 Leave to cool for 10 minutes, then turn onto a cooling rack.

makes 1 loaf

Banana bread

4 oz/125 g butter, at room temperature
1 cup superfine (caster) sugar
2 eggs, lightly beaten
3 ripe bananas, peeled
2 tablespoons honey
2 tablespoons lemon juice
1 teaspoon vanilla extract
1½ cups self-rising (self-raising) flour, sifted
½ teaspoon baking soda
1 teaspoon ground cinnamon
½ cup almond meal

1 Preheat oven to 350°F/180°C. Lightly grease a 9 x 6 in/23 x 15 cm loaf tin.
2 Place butter and sugar in a mixing bowl. Beat with an electric beater until light and creamy. Add eggs and beat until combined.
3 Combine bananas, honey, lemon juice and vanilla in a food processor. Process until smooth.
4 Stir banana mixture into batter and stir until well combined. Gently fold in flour, baking soda, cinnamon and almond meal.
5 Spoon mixture into prepared tin and bake for 50–60 minutes or until cooked. Leave to cool for 5 minutes then place on a wire rack.
6 Cut into slices and serve with butter or place under a grill and serve hot.

serves 8

Fruity carrot loaf

1 cup whole wheat self-rising (wholemeal self-raising) flour
½ cup rye flour
½ cup Demerara (raw) sugar
½ teaspoon salt
½ tablespoon baking soda (bicarbonate of soda)
1 teaspoon ground cinnamon
½ cup crushed pineapple, undrained
1 cup grated carrot
2 eggs

½ cup oil
1 teaspoon vanilla extract
½ cup chopped walnuts

Lemon glacé topping
1 cup confectioners' (icing) sugar
1 teaspoon butter
few drops of vanilla extract
1 tablespoon lemon juice
½ teaspoon lemon zest

1 Preheat oven to 350°F/180°C.
2 Butter an 8 x 6 in/20 x 15 cm loaf tin with melted butter or margarine and line the base with buttered baking paper.
3 Sift the flours, sugar, salt, baking soda and cinnamon into a mixing bowl. Add the crushed pineapple, carrot, eggs, oil and vanilla and beat until well combined. Stir the chopped walnuts into the carrot mixture. Spoon the batter into prepared loaf tin. Bake for 25–30 minutes or until a skewer inserted in the center comes out clean.
4 Remove from the oven and allow to cool in the tin for 5 minutes before turning out onto a wire rack to cool completely.
5 To make lemon glacé topping, place sifted confectioners' sugar in a heat-proof bowl over a pan of simmering water. Make a well in the center of confectioners' sugar, add butter, vanilla extract and 1 tablespoon of lemon juice, and stir slowly until all confectioners' sugar has been incorporated and topping is smooth and shiny. Use while still warm.

makes 1 loaf

Blueberry pecan loaf

9 oz unbleached plain flour
2 teaspoon baking powder
½ teaspoon salt
¼ teaspoon baking soda (bicarbonate of soda)
¼ teaspoon ground nutmeg
4 oz/125 g sugar
2 oz/60 g pecans, chopped
2 eggs
4 tablespoons milk
4 fl oz/125 ml orange juice
2 teaspoons grated orange rind (zest)
3 oz/90 g butter, melted
5 oz/155 g blueberries

1 Preheat the oven to 350°F/180°C. In a large bowl combine flour, baking powder, salt, bicarbonate of soda, nutmeg and sugar. Mix in pecans. Make a well in the centre.
2 In a medium bowl, beat eggs with milk, orange juice and rind. Fold in melted butter. Add egg mixture to flour mixture, mixing until just combined. Gently fold in blueberries.
3 Pour batter into a well-greased 8 x 4 in/20 x 10 cm loaf tin. Bake for 55–65 minutes until loaf is golden and risen. Cool in pan for 10 minutes. Turn onto a wire rack to cool.

makes 1

Traditional scones

2 cups self-rising (self-raising) flour
1 teaspoon baking powder
2 teaspoons sugar
1½ oz/45 g butter
1 egg
½ cup milk

1 Preheat the oven to 430°F/220°C. Sift together flour and baking powder into a large bowl. Stir in sugar, then rub in butter, using fingertips, until mixture resembles coarse breadcrumbs.
2 Whisk together egg and milk. Make a well in the center of the flour mixture, pour in egg mixture and mix to form a soft dough. Turn onto a lightly floured surface and knead lightly.
3 Press dough out to a ¾ in/2 cm thickness, using palm of hand. Cut out scones using a floured 2 in/5 cm cutter. Avoid twisting the cutter, or the scones will rise unevenly.
4 Arrange scones close together on a greased and lightly floured baking tray or in a shallow 8 in/20 cm round cake tin. Brush with a little milk and bake for 12–15 minutes or until golden. Serve with strawberry preserve and whipped cream.

makes 12

Apple loaves

2 cups all-purpose (plain) flour
¼ cup granulated sugar
2 teaspoons baking powder
½ teaspoon baking soda
½ teaspoon salt
1½ oz/45 g butter, chilled
1 large apple, peeled and grated
½ cup milk

1 Preheat oven to 430°F/220°C. Combine flour, sugar, baking powder, baking soda and salt in a large bowl. Cut in butter until crumbly.
2 Add apple and milk. Stir to form soft dough. Turn out on lightly floured surface. Knead gently 8–10 times. Pat into two 10 in/15 cm circles. Place on buttered baking sheet. Brush tops with milk. Sprinkle with sugar, then with cinnamon. Score each top into six pie-shaped wedges. Bake for 15 minutes until browned and risen. Serve warm with butter.

makes 12

Strawberry preserve

4 lb 6 oz/2 kg granulated sugar
4 lb 6 oz/2 kg strawberries, hulled
juice and rind of 2 lemons

1 Warm the sugar in a slow oven. Put the strawberries and lemon in a saucepan and heat gently, stirring as the juice begins to flow out of the fruit. When the juice is coming to the boil, add the warmed sugar.
2 After it has dissolved, bring the preserve to a rapid boil until it thickens and reaches the setting point (about 15–20 minutes).
3 Remove from the heat and let stand for 15 minutes. Ladle into sterilised jars, label and seal.

Note: A perennial favourite, strawberry jelly or jam tastes delicious with warm fresh croissants and tea.

makes 8 lb 13 oz/4 kg

Dry fig preserve

2 lb 3 oz/1 kg dried figs, roughly chopped
8 cups water
rind, pips and juice of 2 lemons
1 teaspoon fennel seeds
3 tablespoons pine nuts
2 oz/60 g flaked almonds
1 lb 10 oz/725 g granulated sugar

1 Soak the dried figs in 1 litre/2 pints of water for several hours.
2 Put the lemon rind and pips into a muslin bag. Place the figs, remaining water, lemon juice and bag of rind and pips in a saucepan and bring to the boil. Simmer until the figs are tender, stirring constantly.
3 Add the fennel seeds, pine nuts, flaked almonds and sugar, then stir until the sugar dissolves. Squeeze the juice out of the muslin bag into the mixture and discard the bag. Boil, stirring constantly, until the setting point is reached.
Ladle the preserve into warm sterilized jars. Label and seal.

Note: This dried fig preserve is very easy to make. It tastes delicious with ice cream, but don't use too much, because it is very rich.

makes 7lb 12 oz/3.5 kg

Raspberry muffins

1 cup whole wheat self-rising (wholemeal self-raising) flour
1 cup white self-rising (self-raising) flour
½ cup bran
½ teaspoon baking soda (bicarbonate of soda)
1 teaspoon ground ginger
¾ cup buttermilk
⅓ cup orange juice concentrate
2 eggs
⅔ cup fresh, or frozen and partly thawed, raspberries

1 Preheat oven to 350°F/180°C. Sift dry ingredients into a bowl. Return any bran to the bowl.
2 Beat together buttermilk, orange juice and eggs. Pour into dry ingredients, all at once. Add raspberries and mix until just combined—take care not to overmix. Spoon into buttered muffin pans.
3 Bake for 20–25 minutes or until cooked when tested with a skewer.

makes 10

Berry crumble muffins

1 cup self-raising (self-rising) flour, sifted
1 cup plain (all-purpose) flour, sifted
1 teaspoon baking powder
½ cup brown sugar
¾ cup milk
¼ cup canola oil
2 eggs, lightly beaten
1 cup frozen mixed berries

Crumble topping
2 tablespoons plain flour
2 tablespoons brown sugar
1 oz/30 g butter, cut into cubes

1 Preheat oven to 350°F/180°C. Butter 12 medium muffin tins.
2 In a medium bowl sift together the flours and baking powder and stir in the sugar.
3 In a separate bowl, mix the milk, oil and eggs together. Make a well in the centre of the
   dry ingredients and pour in the milk mixture.
4 Add the berries and mix until just combined.
5 To make the crumble topping, place the flour and butter in a medium bowl and rub in
   the butter with your fingertips until the mixture resembles breadcrumbs. Stir in the
   sugar and set aside.
6 Spoon the dough into muffin tins and sprinkle with the crumble mixture. Bake for
   20–25 minutes or until muffins are cooked when tested with skewer. Turn onto wire
   racks to cool.

makes 12

Baked eggs

3½ oz/100 g spinach leaves, coarsely chopped
1¾ oz/50 g salted ricotta, sliced
¼ cup thickened cream
2 large eggs

1 Preheat the oven to 375°F/190°C.
2 Place two ramekins in a deep baking tray. Wash the spinach and cook in a medium saucepan over low heat until wilted. Drain off excess water. Transfer the spinach to a medium bowl. Add the ricotta and cream and stir to combine. Spoon the spinach mixture into the ramekins and break an egg into the centre.
3 Fill the baking tray with boiling water to come halfway up the sides of the ramekins. Bake in the oven for 15 minutes, or until the eggs have set.

serves 2

Creamed spinach & egg on toast

7 oz/200 g spinach, washed and chopped
½ cup thickened cream
2 large eggs
2 slices multigrain bread, about 1 in/2 cm thick

1 Place the cream and spinach in a large saucepan on medium heat. Cook for 5–10 minutes until the cream has thickened to a saucy consistency.
2 Meanwhile, bring a medium saucepan of water to the simmer. Using a spoon, create a whirlpool and crack the eggs one at a time into the centre. Poach for about 3 minutes, or until whites are slightly firm.
3 Cook the bread in a toaster until golden brown. Arrange the toast, creamed spinach and eggs onto two serving plates.

serves 2

Poached eggs on toast

4 large eggs
2 slices sourdough bread, about 1 in/2 cm thick
⅓ cup beetroot chutney
1¾ oz/50 g arugula (rocket) leaves

1 Bring a medium saucepan of water to the simmer. Using a spoon, create a whirlpool and crack the eggs one at a time into the centre. Poach for about 3 minutes or until whites are slightly firm.
2 Cook the bread in a toaster until golden brown. Arrange the toast, eggs, rocket and chutney onto two serving plates.

serves 2

Eggs benedict

8 English muffins, toasted
2 tablespoons butter, softened
8 thin slices ham
8 poached eggs
1 tablespoon caviar
1 lime, cut into wedges

Hollandaise sauce
4 oz/125 g butter
4 egg yolks
1½ tablespoons lemon juice
salt and freshly ground black pepper

1 To make Hollandaise sauce, cut butter into thirds. Place egg yolks and one-third of the butter in a double boiler and cook over hot, but not boiling, water until butter melts, stirring quickly.
2 Add the next next third of butter, still stirring. The mixture will start to thicken, then add the last third of butter. When butter is melted, remove pan from hot water and stir quickly for about 2 minutes. Stir in the lemon juice, a teaspoon at a time, then add salt and pepper.
3 Heat again over hot water, stirring constantly. When heated, remove immediately.
4 Spread toast with a little butter, then top each piece with a slice of ham, a poached egg and Hollandaise sauce. Serve with a little caviar on top and a wedge of lime.

serves 4

Fried eggs & bacon

1 tablespoon butter
8 eggs
8 rashers bacon
4 tomatoes, sliced

1 Heat a large non-stick frying pan. Add the bacon and fry until some fat is released into the pan. Add the tomatoes and continue cooking until golden brown on both sides.
2 Heat butter over a low heat, crack eggs into a bowl and slide gently into the pan. Cover the pan and cook for 1 minute, take off the lid and baste the eggs with butter, then replace lid for about 2 minutes or until white is firm. If your frying pan has no lid just baste with the butter until desired consistency.
3 Serve eggs with bacon and tomatoes.

serves 4

Breakfast feast

8 rashers bacon
4 tomatoes, halved
2 onions, thinly sliced
4 lean beef sausages
2 teaspoons white vinegar
1 tablespoon plain flour
salt and freshly ground black pepper
8 large free-range eggs, at room temperature
4 slices Turkish bread, toasted

1 Dry-fry the bacon and tomato pieces in a non-stick frying pan, then place in a warm oven. Fry the onions in the same pan with the sausages. Cook for 8 minutes, turning a few times.
2 Sprinkle the flour over the sausages and onion, stirring well. Add ½ cup of hot water and salt and pepper to taste. Cover and simmer for 5 minutes.
3 Meanwhile, half-fill a separate large frying pan with water and bring to a simmer. Add the vinegar.
4 Swirl the simmering frying pan with a large spoon, to create a gentle whirlpool motion. Crack the eggs into the centre of the water and gently swirl the water again. After the water returns to the simmer, wait 2 minutes longer and gently remove and drain the poached eggs. Serve eggs on top of Turkish bread with bacon, tomato, sauage and onion at the side.

serves 4

Sausages & grilled tomato

4 pork and fennel sausages
2 large ripe tomatoes, thickly sliced
4 tablespoons basil pesto
2 slices sourdough bread, about 1 in/2 cm thick

1 Preheat the grill to medium.
2 Place the sausages on a grill tray and cook, turning occasionally, for 15 minutes
   or until cooked.
3 Meanwhile, place the tomatoes on a small baking tray and spread with pesto. Cook
   under the grill for 5–10 minutes until they begin to soften. Toast the bread under the
   grill or in a toaster until golden brown.
4 Arrange the toast, sausages and tomatoes onto two serving plates.

serves 2

Poached eggs in spinach

1½ oz/40 g butter
½ bunch scallions (spring onions)
1 lb/500 g frozen English spinach, thawed
¼ cup fresh dill, chopped
1 tablespoon lemon juice
salt and freshly ground black pepper
2 oz/60 g feta cheese, crumbled
4 eggs

1 Heat butter in a frying pan over low heat, add the spring onions and stir to coat. Cover with a lid and cook slowly for 5 minutes.
2 Add the spinach, dill and lemon juice and mix well. Increase heat to moderately high and cook 3–4 minutes. Stir in salt, pepper and crumbled cheese.
3 Make 4 depressions in the spinach and break an egg into each. Cover and cook on moderate heat until eggs are set. Serve immediately.

serves 4

Scrambled eggs

8 eggs
⅔ cup milk
salt and freshly ground black pepper
1 oz/30 g butter

1 Beat the eggs lightly and add milk, salt and pepper.
2 Heat the butter in a frying pan, add the beaten eggs and stir continuously with a wooden spoon until a creamy texture. Do not have the heat too high.

Note: Scrambled eggs can become a gourmet meal with imaginative additives as follows:
   • Chopped chives or parsley and crisp bacon crumbles
   • Sliced mushrooms, previously fried in butter
   • Skin and grill a tomato and chop finely
   • Finely grated orange zest
   • Dice cooked potatoes, fried to golden brown
   • Soak anchovies in milk, drain, slice and add.

serves 4

Ham & cheese croissant

2 croissants, halved crosswise
2 slices honey-cured ham
4 slices fontina cheese
3 tablespoons tomato chutney

1 Preheat the grill to high.
2 Grill the croissants on both sides until golden.
3 Lay the ham slices on the bottom halves and top with cheese. Cook under the grill until the cheese has melted. Spread on the chutney, place the croissant lids on top and serve.

serves 2

Smoked salmon bagel

⅓ cup cream cheese
freshly ground black pepper
2 teaspoons horseradish cream
3½ oz/100 g smoked salmon
1 lime
4 bagels
1 red onion, sliced
2 teaspoons capers
2 oz/60 g mixed lettuce leaves
½ cup cherry tomatoes, halved

1 Combine the cream cheese, black pepper and horseradish cream and mix well.
2 Separate the smoked salmon slices and squeeze over the juice of half the lime.
3 Toast the halved bagels and spread the cream cheese mixture onto each one. Top with slices of smoked salmon, red onion slices and a few capers.
4 Toss the lettuce and tomatoes with a squeeze of lime and serve as an accompaniment to the salmon bagels.

Note: Wasabi or mustard also work very well instead of the horseradish cream.

serves 4

Potato rösti with smoked trout

14 oz/400 g sebago potatoes, washed
1½ oz/45 g butter, melted
1¾ oz/50 g watercress
½ smoked trout, bones and skin removed

1 Place the unpeeled potatoes in a medium saucepan. Cover with cold water and bring to the boil. Cook for 10 minutes, drain and allow to cool completely. Peel and grate the potatoes and place in a medium bowl. Add the melted butter and toss to combine.
2 Preheat a large non-stick frying pan over medium-high heat. Place two mounds of potato onto the pan and flatten with a spatula. Cook for 10 minutes on both sides or until golden brown and crisp. Place röstis onto two serving plates. Top with watercress and smoked trout.

serves 2

Potato and zucchini rösti

1 lb/500 g potatoes, peeled and grated
10½ oz/300 g zucchini, grated
2 eggs, lightly beaten
¼ cup all-purpose (plain) flour
1 teaspoons dill leaf tips
salt and freshly ground black pepper
oil for cooking
½ cup light cream cheese
2 teaspoons lemon pepper seasoning
baby rocket leaves
7 oz/200 g smoked salmon, cut into pieces
2 tablespoons capers

1 Place the potatoes and zucchini in a colander and squeeze out the liquid.
2 Combine the potatoes, zucchini, eggs, flour, dill, salt and pepper in a bowl.
3 Heat 1 teaspoon oil at a time in a large frying pan over low to medium heat. Add ¼ cup mixture and flatten. Cook each rösti for 2–3 minutes on each side or until golden and cooked. Remove and set aside. Repeat with the remaining oil and mixture.
4 Combine the cream cheese and lemon pepper seasoning in a bowl. Mix well.
5 Spread the rösti with cream cheese. Top with rocket leaves, salmon and capers.

Note: When you grate the potato and zucchini you need to squeeze out the excess water otherwise the rösti are soggy when cooked. You can vary the recipe by using smoked trout instead of smoked salmon.

makes 12

Smoked turkey open sandwich

1 tablespoon (20 ml) whole egg mayonnaise
12 slices (approx. 6½ oz/200 g) smoked turkey
6 mini bagels, halved
salt and black pepper
2 tablespoons cranberry jelly
a handful of baby rocket leaves

1 Spread the mayonnaise evenly on each bagel half.
2 Put a slice of folded turkey on each bagel.
3 Season well with salt and black pepper.
4 Smear a teaspoon of cranberry jelly across the turkey.
5 Top with a few leaves of rocket (about 5 on each).
6 Serve on a large platter.

makes 12

Egg and cress fingers

2 hard boiled eggs
1 tablespoon mayonnaise
salt and pepper
4 slices soft white fresh bread, lightly buttered
½ small punnet (approx. 3½ oz/100 g) mustard cress (or use finely shredded iceberg
   lettuce, watercress or snow pea sprouts)

1 Slice and fork the eggs together with mayonnaise, salt and pepper to make a coarse
   mixture.
2 Spread evenly across two slices of fresh bread.
3 Top one slice with scattered mustard cress and place other slice on top.
4 Trim crusts off sandwich and cut into three fingers, then cut each finger in half.

makes 6

Smoked salmon & cucumber

1 tablespoon whole egg mayonnaise
2 teaspoons (approx. 16) baby capers, chopped
1 teaspoon chopped fresh dill
4 slices soft white fresh bread, lightly buttered
1½–3½ oz/50–100 g smoked salmon (or smoked trout)
¼ small or English cucumber, finely sliced
black pepper

1 Combine the mayonnaise, chopped capers and dill and spread on the two slices of fresh bread.
2 Place the smoked salmon generously on top.
3 Overlap nine thin slices of cucumber until they are covering the salmon.
4 Season with freshly ground black pepper.
5 Top with second slice of fresh bread.
6 Trim crusts off sandwich and cut into three fingers, then cut each finger in half.

makes 6

Smoked trout with lime

1 tablespoon softened cream cheese
2 teaspoons whole egg mayonnaise
½ lime
salt and black pepper
4 slices soft wholemeal fresh bread, lightly buttered
50–100 g (1½–3½ oz) smoked ocean trout

1 Combine the cream cheese and mayonnaise.
2 Add the juice and grated peel of ½ lime. The mixture needs to be quite stiff, so do not
   add all the lime juice if this makes it runny.
3 Season with salt and pepper to taste.
4 Spread quite thickly onto two slices of fresh bread.
5 Top with slices of ocean trout and second slice of fresh bread.
6 Trim the crusts and cut each into four neat triangles.

makes 8

Crab, chives & celery sandwich

¼ stick celery, very finely chopped
½ tablespoon crème fraîche
2 garlic chives (or ordinary chives), finely chopped
70 g/2½ oz crabmeat
salt and black pepper
4 slices soft white bread, lightly buttered

1 Mix the celery with the crème fraîche and chives.
2 Add the crabmeat, gently stirring to combine. Season well with salt and pepper.
3 Spread the mixture onto two slices of fresh bread.
4 Top with second slice of bread.
5 Trim the crusts and cut into three fingers, then cut each finger in half.

makes 6

Chicken & walnut

½ tablespoon cream cheese, softened
½ tablespoon mayonnaise
1 tablespoon milk
a handful of walnuts, finely chopped
½ poached chicken breast (approx. 3½ oz/100 g), shredded
1 tablespoon flat-leaf parsley, chopped
salt and black pepper
4 slices soft wholemeal fresh bread, lightly buttered

1 Mix the cream cheese and mayonnaise together. If a more liquid consistency is needed to coat the chicken, add a small quantity of milk.
2 Stir the walnuts into the mayonnaise mixture.
3 Add the shredded chicken and chopped parsley, and mix to combine. Season to taste.
4 Divide the mixture onto two slices of fresh bread and top with the other slices.
5 Trim crusts off sandwich and cut into three fingers, then cut each finger in half.

makes 6

Steak sandwich deluxe

1 long loaf Turkish bread
4 minute-steaks
salt and freshly ground black pepper
1 tablespoon oil
1 onion, thinly sliced
2 tablespoons steak sauce or barbecue sauce
4 large button mushrooms, thinly sliced
1 red capsicum, cut into thin strips
4 slices aged Cheddar cheese

1 Cut the Turkish bread into 4 pieces, then split each through the centre.
2 Pound the minute-steaks a little thinner with a meat mallet and sprinkle with salt and pepper. Brush the steaks with a little oil, place in a frying pan and cook for 2–3 minutes each side.
3 Place the steaks onto the base slices of the Turkish bread, top with the onion and drizzle with sauce. Place the mushrooms and capsicum on top, then a slice of cheese.
4 Place the sandwiches under the griller, and place the top slices of Turkish bread next to the sandwiches. Grill for 2–3 minutes until the cheese melts and the top slices are lightly toasted. Remove from grill and place the top slices on top of the sandwiches. Wrap the ends in a strip of baking paper for easy eating and serve immediately.

serves 4

Herb blinis with salmon roe

1 cup self-raising (self-rising) flour, sifted
1 egg, lightly beaten
¾ cup milk
1 tablespoon finely chopped dill
2 teaspoons thinly sliced chives
salt and freshly ground black pepper
butter for cooking
⅔ cup light sour cream
½ teaspoon finely grated lemon rind
2 oz/60 g jar salmon roe

1 Combine flour, egg, milk, dill, chives, salt and pepper in a mixing bowl. Whisk together until smooth.
2 Heat a little butter in a nonstick frying pan. Add spoonfuls of mixture in batches (about 2 in/5 cm in diameter). Cook for 1–2 minutes each side or until golden.
3 Combine sour cream and lemon rind in a small bowl. Top blinis with a dollop of sour cream and a little salmon roe.

makes about 24

Smoked fish & egg turnovers

5 oz/150 g smoked ocean trout portion, skin removed and flaked
2 hardboiled eggs, chopped
½ cup cooked long-grain rice
1 tablespoon chopped dill
2 tablespoons finely chopped dill pickle
2 scallions (spring onions), sliced
salt and freshly ground black pepper
6 sheets puff or shortcrust pastry, thawed
1 egg, lightly beaten

1 Preheat oven to 430°F/220°C.
2 Line a baking tray with baking paper.
3 Combine fish, hardboiled eggs, rice, dill, dill pickle, shallots, salt and pepper in a bowl.
4 Cut puff pastry into 4 in/10 cm rounds. Place a heaped tablespoon of mixture in the centre. Brush the edges with water and press together. Pinch the edges together and place upright on prepared baking tray.
5 Brush pastries with beaten egg and bake in the oven for about 15 minutes or until golden and puffed.

makes about 24

Tofu burgers

12 oz/350 g firm tofu
1 tablespoon olive oil
1 clove garlic, crushed
2 teaspoons ground cummin
salt and freshly ground black pepper
4 slices crusty bread or bread rolls
4 tablespoons hummus
2 oz/60 g mixed salad leaves
1 red capsicum, finely chopped

1 Cut tofu into 4 even slices.
2 Combine oil, garlic, cummin and seasoning in a bowl. Dip tofu slices in the mix and coat well. Pan-fry the tofu until heated through, about 2 minutes each side.
3 Serve on crusty bread or bread rolls spread with hummus, top with mixed salad leaves and chopped capsicum.

serves 4

Bacon and avocado muffin

4 rashers bacon, halved and rind removed
2 English muffins, halved crosswise
2 tablespoons mayonnaise
1 ripe avocado, halved and stone removed

1 Preheat a medium non-stick frying pan on medium-high heat. Cook the bacon for 2 minutes on each side or until crisp.
2 Toast the muffins in a toaster until golden brown. Spread mayonnaise on the muffin tops.
3 Slice the avocado and lay on the base of the muffins. Top with bacon slices and cover with muffin tops.

serves 2

Mixed mushrooms on muffins

12 oz/350 g mixed mushrooms, including wild, oyster and shiitake
2 tablespoons olive oil
salt and freshly ground black pepper
1 tablespoon butter
1 clove garlic, crushed
¼ cup fresh parsley, chopped
½ small bunch chives, chopped
2 teaspoon sherry vinegar or balsamic vinegar
1½ oz/40 g low-fat soft cheese
2 English white muffins

1 Halve any large mushrooms. Heat 2 teaspoons of the oil in a heavy-based frying pan, then add the mushrooms, season lightly and fry over a medium to high heat for 5 minutes or until they start to release their juices.
2 Remove the mushrooms and drain on absorbent paper, then set aside. Add the rest of the oil and half the butter to the pan and heat until the butter melts. Add the garlic and stir for 1 minute.
3 Return the mushrooms to the pan, then increase the heat to high and fry for 5 minutes or until they are tender and starting to crisp. Stir in the remaining butter and 1 tablespoon each of parsley and chives, drizzle with the vinegar and season.
4 Mix the soft cheese with the remaining parsley and chives. Split and toast the muffins. Spread the soft cheese mixture over the muffin halves and place on serving plates. Top with the mushrooms and garnish with whole chives.

Note: Make sure the mushrooms are piping hot when you pile them onto the muffins—that way, they'll start to melt into the soft cheese, which in turn will fuse with the bread.

serves 4

Grilled mushrooms

7 oz/200 g baby spinach leaves
4 large field mushrooms, stalks trimmed
3½ oz/100 g feta cheese, crumbled
¼ cup sun-dried tomato pesto

1 Preheat the grill to high.
2 Wash the spinach and cook in a medium saucepan over low heat until wilted.
3 Place the mushrooms on a baking tray stem-side down and grill for 3 minutes.
4 Turn the mushrooms over and top with wilted spinach. Sprinkle with feta and pesto.
   Grill for a further 3 minutes, until mushrooms are cooked and cheese is golden.

serves 2

Papaya fruit salad

½ papaya, peeled
1 orange, peeled
2 kiwifruit, peeled
1 small banana, peeled
¼ pineapple, skin removed
small bunch green grapes
small bunch red grapes
7 oz/200 g strawberries
2 passionfruit
2 sprigs mint
juice of 1 lemon
2 tablespoons Grand Marnier

1 Cut the papaya into small cubes, cut the orange into segments, and cut kiwifruit into thin slices. Slice the banana into medium-size slices and dice the pineapple into cubes (do not use the pineapple core).
2 Gently combine all cut fruit with the grapes, strawberries and passionfruit pulp.
3 Separate the mint leaves and pour the lemon juice over the fruit salad.
4 Pour over Grand Marnier and scatter with mint leaves. Serve as a centrepiece on a buffet table or in hearty individual serves.

Note: The secret to this dish is the addition of lemon juice, which brings out the flavour of the papaya.

serves 4

Omelettes

Asparagus omelette

2 eggs
freshly ground black pepper
1 tablespoon butter
3 canned asparagus spears, drained, or 3 fresh asparagus spears,
  trimmed and cooked until tender

1 Place eggs, 1 tablespoon of water and black pepper to taste in a bowl and whisk to combine.
2 Melt butter in an omelette pan over a medium heat. Add egg mixture to pan and cook, continually drawing the edge of the omelette in with a fork until no liquid remains and the omelette is lightly set.
3 Place asparagus spears in centre of omelette, fold omelette and slide onto a plate. Serve immediately.

serves 1

Bean sprout omelette

Filling
2 tablespoons butter
2 in/5 cm piece fresh ginger, grated
4 tablespoons bean sprouts
4 chives, finely chopped

Omelette
1 teaspoon butter
2 eggs
freshly ground black pepper

1 To make the filling, melt the butter in a small frying pan. Add ginger, bean sprouts and chives and cook for 1 minute. Remove from the pan and keep warm.
2 To make the omelette, melt the butter in a small frying pan. Lightly whisk together the eggs, and 2 teaspoons of water and season with pepper. Pour into the pan and cook over a medium heat. Continually draw the edge of the omelette in with a fork during cooking until no liquid remains and the omelette is lightly set.
3 Sprinkle the bean sprout mixture over the omelette and fold in half. Slip onto a plate and serve immediately.

serves 1

Blue cheese omelette

1 tablespoon butter
2 eggs
freshly ground black pepper

Cheese and apple filling
1 tablespoon butter
½ small green apple, cored and thinly sliced
1 oz/30 g blue cheese, crumbled
4 chives, snipped

1 To make filling, melt butter in a small frying pan and cook apple over a low heat for 2–3
   minutes or until just heated through. Remove pan from heat, set aside and keep warm.
2 To make omelette, melt butter in a small frying pan. Place eggs, 2 teaspoons of water
   and black pepper to taste in a small bowl and whisk to combine. Pour egg mixture into
   frying pan and cook over a medium heat continually drawing in the edge of the omelette
   with a fork during cooking, until no liquid remains and the omelette is lightly set.
3 Top half the omelette with apple slices, cheese and chives and fold in half. Slip onto a
   plate and serve immediately.

serves 1

Basil & feta omelette

4 large eggs, separated
½ cup fresh basil leaves, torn
3 oz/90 g feta cheese, crumbled
½ red onion, sliced

1 Preheat the grill to medium-high. Beat the egg yolks in a medium bowl. In a separate bowl, whisk the whites until soft peaks form. Gently fold the whites through the yolks until combined.
2 Preheat a small non-stick frying pan on medium heat. Spoon half the egg mixture into the pan and cook for 1 minute. Place the pan under the hot grill and cook the top of the omelette for a further 1–2 minutes or until set and golden. Set aside and keep warm. Repeat the process for the remaining egg mixture.
3 Serve topped with basil, feta and red onion.

serves 2

French omelette

2 eggs
freshly ground black pepper
1 tablespoon butter

1 Place eggs, 2 tablespoons of water and black pepper to taste in a bowl and whisk lightly to combine.
2 Heat an omelette pan over a medium heat until hot. Add butter, tipping the pan so the base is completely coated. Heat until the butter is foaming, but not browned, then add the egg mixture. As it sets, use a palette knife or fork to gently draw up the edge of the omelette until no liquid remains and the omelette is lightly set.
3 Serve omelette plain, or topped with filling of your choice, and fold in half. Slip omelette onto a plate and serve immediately.

serves 1

Kukuye sabsi

1 large potato, peeled and diced
olive oil
4–5 scallions (spring onions), chopped
1 lb/500 g silverbeet or spinach leaves
6 eggs, beaten
1 cup flat-leaf parsley, chopped
½ bunch chives, snipped
salt and freshly ground pepper
juice of ½ a lemon

1 Preheat oven to 350°F/180°C. Fry the potato in a little olive oil in a large frying pan until pale golden. Add the chopped spring onions and cook, stirring, until softened. If using silverbeet, remove all the white stalks and chop the leaves finely. Combine the chopped silverbeet or spinach with the egg and add the cooked potato and onion mixture along with the remaining ingredients. Mix well.

2 Grease a shallow ovenproof dish and pour in the mixture. Bake for 35 minutes, covering the dish for the first 20 minutes. The vegetables should be tender and the eggs set with a golden crust. Alternatively the kukuye can be cooked in a frying pan, like the Spanish tortilla. When the eggs have set underneath, the top can be drizzled with a little melted butter or oil and browned under the grill. Offer a bowl of yoghurt with the kukuye.

serves 4

Leek omelette

1 lb/500 g leeks
butter for frying
a good squeeze of lemon juice
salt and freshly ground black pepper
4 large eggs

1 Cut off the tough tops of the leeks and remove the outer leaves. Make a slit down one side of the leeks and wash the leaves, leaving the leeks whole. Now slice the leeks fairly thinly. Melt a little butter in a frying pan and fry the leeks lightly for a few minutes. Add the lemon juice, salt and pepper and continue cooking over a gentle heat until the leeks are tender and lightly coloured.

2 Beat the eggs lightly in a bowl, pour in the leek mixture and stir to mix. Heat more butter in the pan and when sizzling add the egg and leek mixture. Cook over a gentle heat for about 10 minutes or until the eggs are set and the underside is golden. Check this frequently by lifting the edge carefully with a spatula. Invert a plate over the frying pan and turn out the omelette. Return to the pan, uncooked side down, and cook until golden and completely set. Turn out on to a serving dish and cut into wedges to serve. Alternatively, the uncooked top can be browned under a hot grill.

serves 4

Pickled vegetable omelette

2 tablespoons peanut or groundnut oil
8 oz/250 g lean beef mince
2 tablespoons bottled Chinese mixed vegetables (tung chai), drained and chopped
1 teaspoon honey
2 tablespoons soy sauce
6 scallions (spring onions), finely chopped
6 eggs, lightly beaten

1 Heat 1 tablespoon oil in a frying pan and stir-fry beef mince, vegetables, honey, soy sauce and spring onions for 3–4 minutes or until cooked. Remove from pan, set aside and keep warm.
2 Heat remaining oil in a clean frying pan, pour in one-quarter of the beaten eggs. Swirl pan over heat to make a thin omelette. Spoon one-quarter of the meat mixture into the centre of the omelette and fold over the edges.
3 Remove omelette from pan, set aside and keep warm. Repeat with remaining eggs and meat mixture. Cut omelette into slices and serve immediately.

serves 4

Potato & pea omelette

1 teaspoon vegetable oil or butter
1 small slice ham, chopped
1 small potato, finely chopped
1–2 tablespoons peas or sweet corn kernels
1 egg, lightly beaten
2 tablespoons milk

1 Heat the oil or butter in a small frying pan over a medium heat. Add the ham, potato and peas or sweet corn and cook, stirring frequently for 5–10 minutes or until the potato is tender.
2 Place the egg and milk in a bowl and whisk to combine. Pour the egg mixture over the potato mixture in pan, reduce the heat and cook without stirring for 3–4 minutes or until the omelette is just firm.

serves 1

Shrimp & cucumber omelette

8 eggs

Shrimp and cucumber filling
½ cup chicken stock
1 tablespoon rice wine or dry sherry
1 tablespoon oyster sauce
2 teaspoons light soy sauce
2 tablespoons peanut oil
2 in/5 cm piece fresh ginger, finely chopped
3 large shallots, sliced
1 clove garlic, crushed
⅔ cup tiny peeled shrimp (prawns)
1 small cucumber, peeled, seeded and diced
2 teaspoons cornflour mixed with 1 teaspoon water
1 teaspoon sesame oil

1 Whisk the eggs and 4 tablespoons of water together. Heat oil in a small frying pan. Use the mixture to make 4 omelettes. Once cooked, keep warm while you prepare the filling.
2 In a small bowl, combine the chicken stock, rice wine, oyster and soy sauces. Heat the peanut oil over a moderately high heat, add the chopped ginger, shallots and garlic and quickly sauté for 1 minute. Add the shrimp and toss for a minute, then add the cucumber and cook for another 30 seconds.
3 Add the sauce mixture and cook for 2 minutes. Add the cornflour mixture and cook for 30 seconds or so until slightly thickened. Remove from the heat and stir in the sesame oil. Spoon into omelettes before folding and rolling.

serves 4

Smoked salmon omelette

4 eggs
2 tablespoons milk
2 teaspoons dried chopped chives
4 oz/125 g smoked salmon
2 tablespoons sour cream

1 Whisk together eggs, milk and chives in a bowl and season with salt and pepper.
2 Heat a small non-stick fry pan over low heat. Pour in half the egg mixture and cook for about 4–5 minutes or until egg is nearly set.
3 Place half the smoked salmon over one half of the omelette. Top with 1 tablespoon sour cream and fold over.
4 Remove omelette and repeat with remaining ingredients.

serves 2

Spring omelette

1 tablespoon butter
4 eggs, lightly beaten
3 tablespoons milk
freshly ground black pepper
3 tablespoons grated mature Cheddar cheese

Vegetable filling
1 tablespoon butter
2 scallions (spring onions), finely chopped
6 button mushrooms, sliced
½ small red bell pepper (capsicum), cut into thin strips
¼ cup fresh cilantro (coriander), chopped

1 To make filling, melt butter in a frying pan and cook spring onions, mushrooms, red capsicum and coriander for 2 minutes or until vegetables are tender. Remove vegetables from pan, set aside and keep warm.
2 Melt butter in a clean frying pan. Place eggs, milk and black pepper to taste in a bowl and whisk to combine. Pour egg mixture into pan. As the omelette cooks, use a palette knife or fork to gently draw up the edge of the omelette until no liquid remains and the omelette is lightly set. Top half the omelette with filling, then sprinkle with cheese. Fold omelette over, cut in half, slide onto serving plates and serve immediately.

serves 2

Tomato & basil omelette

3 eggs
salt and freshly ground black pepper
½ cup parsley, chopped
3 tablespoons butter

1 tablespoon Parmesan cheese, grated
1 tablespoon light cream
½ tomato, seeded
¼ bunch fresh basil, leaves picked

1 To make the filling, melt one tablespoon of the butter in the omelette pan. Add the tomatoes and basil and heat for one minute. Remove from pan and keep warm.
2 Break the eggs into a bowl and season with salt and pepper. Add 1 tablespoon of water and half the parsley, and beat with a fork just enough to mix the yolks and whites together.
3 Heat an 8 in/20 cm omelette or frying pan until hot enough to make the butter sizzle on contact. Add one tablespoon of the butter to the heated pan and shake gently so that the butter coats the pan evenly.
4 When the butter sizzles but is not turning brown, pour in the egg mixture all at once. Quickly stir for a second or two to ensure even cooking. As the egg starts to set, lift the edges with a fork so the liquid can run underneath. Repeat until all the liquid is used up but the eggs are still moist and soft.
5 Sprinkle the tomato/basil mixture over the omelette, tilt the pan away from you and loosen around the edges if necessary. Allow the omelette to slip up the far edge of the pan, then fold top half over away from the handle. Slide the omelette on to a warm plate by tilting the pan and raising the handle to release the omelette just as it touches the plate. Melt the remaining butter, toss in the remaining parsley and pour over the omelette. Serve immediately.

serves 1

Quiches and Flans

Asparagus & pasta quiche

3 oz/90 g small pasta shapes
1 tablespoon salt
2 sheets pre-made shortcrust pastry
4 oz/125 g Gruyère cheese, thinly sliced
12 oz/340 g canned asparagus tips, well drained
3 small eggs
1 cup double cream
pinch grated nutmeg
freshly ground black pepper

1 Place the pasta in lots of boiling water in a large saucepan with salt and cook for
   8 minutes, or until just firm in the centre (al dente). Drain, set aside and keep warm.
2 Preheat the oven to 350°F/180°C. Roll out the pastry to ⅛ in/5 mm thick and use it to
   line a 8 in/20 cm spring-form tin. Prick the base and sides of the pastry case with a fork,
   line with baking paper and half-fill with uncooked rice. Bake for 15 minutes or until pastry
   is lightly browned. Remove paper and rice and set pastry case aside to cool.
3 Arrange the cheese over the pastry base and top with asparagus and pasta.
4 Place eggs, cream, nutmeg and black pepper to taste in a bowl and whisk to combine.
   Carefully pour egg mixture into pastry case and bake for 30 minutes, until filling is firm.
   Serve hot, warm or cold.

serves 4

Blue cheese & onion quiche

13 oz/370 g prepared shortcrust pastry
2 tablespoons butter
3 onions, thinly sliced
2 cloves garlic, crushed
3 eggs
2 oz/60 g blue cheese, crumbled
1 cup milk
¾ cup sour cream
freshly ground black pepper
2 teaspoons caraway seeds

1 Roll pastry to fit a 9 in/23 cm fluted flan tin. Place a sheet of greaseproof paper over pastry, and half-fill with rice. Bake in moderately hot oven for 8 minutes. Remove rice and paper, bake further 10 minutes or until golden brown.
2 Melt butter in a frying pan, add onion and garlic and stir-fry over low heat for about 10 minutes, or until onions are soft and golden brown. Spoon evenly over pastry.
3 Preheat oven to 315°F/160°C. Lightly beat eggs, then add cheese, milk, sour cream, pepper and caraway seeds and gently pour over onions.
4 Bake in oven for 30 minutes or until just set and lightly browned.

serves 4

Wholemeal spinach quiche

Wholemeal pastry

2 cups wholemeal flour, sifted and husks
  returned
4 tablespoons olive oil
2 eggs, lightly beaten

Spinach filling

2 tablespoons butter
1 onion, finely chopped

8 oz/250 g spinach, stalks removed and
  leaves finely shredded
2 oz/60 g mature Cheddar cheese, grated
1¼ cups sour cream
3 eggs, lightly beaten
pinch ground nutmeg
freshly ground black pepper

1 Preheat oven to 440°F/220°C. To make pastry, combine oil, egg and one tablespoon of iced water. Place flour in a food processor. With machine running, add oil mixture to flour and process to make a firm dough. Turn dough onto a lightly floured surface and knead briefly. Wrap in plastic food wrap and chill for 30 minutes.

2 Roll out pastry to ⅕ in/5 mm thick and use to line the base and sides of a lightly greased 9 in/23 cm flan tin. Trim edges. Line pastry case with baking paper, half-fill with uncooked rice and bake for 15 minutes. Remove rice and paper and bake for 10 minutes longer. Set aside to cool.

3 To make filling, melt butter in a frying pan over a medium heat, add onion and cook for 4–5 minutes or until soft. Stir in spinach and cook for 2–3 minutes or until spinach wilts. Set aside to cool.

4 Place cheese, sour cream, eggs, nutmeg and black pepper to taste in a bowl and mix to combine. Spread spinach mixture over pastry base, then carefully pour over egg mixture. Reduce oven temperature to 350°F/180°C and bake for 30 minutes or until filling is firm.

serves 6

Corn & ham quiche

4 oz/125 g prepared shortcrust pastry
4 oz/125 g canned sweetcorn kernels, drained
4 oz/125 g ham, chopped
3 scallions (spring onions), finely chopped
3 oz/90 g mature Cheddar cheese, grated
¾ cup sour cream
½ cup milk
3 eggs

1 Preheat oven to 400°F/200°C. Roll out pastry and use to line a lightly greased
   9 in/3 cm flan tin. Prick pastry with a fork, line with baking paper and fill with uncooked
   rice. Bake for 5 minutes, then remove rice and paper and bake for 10 minutes longer
   or until pastry is golden.
2 Place sweetcorn, ham, spring onions and cheese in a bowl and mix to combine. Spread
   sweetcorn mixture over base of pastry case. Place sour cream, milk and eggs in a bowl
   and beat to combine.
3 Pour over sweetcorn mixture, reduce oven temperature to 350°F/180°C and bake for
   30 minutes or until top is golden and filling firm.

serves 6

Corn & kibble quiche

10 slices multigrain bread, crusts removed
2½ oz/75 g butter, melted
1 onion, finely chopped
4 oz/125 g button mushrooms, sliced
freshly ground black pepper
4 eggs, beaten
¾ cup double cream
11 oz/315 g canned corn kernels, drained

1 Preheat oven to 350°F/180°C. Use 1 tablespoon of melted butter to brush over both sides of bread slices. Line a 9 in/23 cm pie plate or quiche tin with bread, pressing firmly to the edges. Bake for 10 minutes or until set and pale golden, remove and set aside to cool.
2 Heat remaining butter in a frying pan over a medium heat, add onion and mushrooms and cook, stirring for 2–3 minutes or until onion is just coloured.Remove pan from heat, season with black pepper to taste and set aside to cool slightly.
3 Place eggs, cream and corn in a bowl and mix to combine. Add mushroom mixture, mix well and pour into prepared bread case. Bake for 30–40 minutes or until filling is set. Serve hot or cold with a crisp, green salad.

serves 4–6

Feta quiche

Shortcrust pastry
1 cups all-purpose (plain) flour, sifted
½ teaspoon salt
7 oz/200 g butter, cold, cut into pieces
⅓ cup lard, cold, cut into pieces

Filling
7 oz/200 g feta cheese, crumbled

7 oz/200 g cream cheese, softened
2 eggs
1 tablespoon fresh basil, chopped
2 sprigs rosemary, leaves picked and
 finely chopped
½ cup sour cream
freshly ground black pepper

1 Preheat oven to 400°F/200°C. To make shortcrust pastry, place flour, salt, butter and lard in a food processor. Process until mixture resembles coarse breadcrumbs. With machine running, add water and process until dough forms a ball.

2 Remove to a lightly floured surface and flatten ball with your hand. Wrap in plastic wrap and refrigerate 30 minutes.

3 On a lightly floured surface, roll dough out to line a 9 in/23 cm quiche dish and prick the pastry all over with a fork. Line with baking paper and half-fill with uncooked rice. Bake for 15 minutes, or until the pastry is lightly browned. Reduce oven heat to 360°C/180°C.

4 In the clean bowl of the food processor, combine feta, cream cheese, eggs, basil, rosemary and sour cream. Blend until smooth and creamy. Season to taste with freshly ground black pepper.

5 Pour into pastry case and bake until custard has set, about 50 minutes. Remove from oven and stand at least 30 minutes at room temperature.

serves 12–16

Individual sweet potato quiche

2 sheets prepared shortcrust pastry, thawed
1 tablespoon olive oil
2 teaspoons butter
1 large brown onion, halved and thinly sliced
1 sweet potato, about 10 oz/300 g, peeled and cut into 1 in/2.5 cm pieces
¾ cup thickened cream
3 eggs, lightly whisked
¼ cup basil, chopped

1 Cut circles from the pastry and press into a 12-cup muffin tray. Refrigerate for 15 minutes.
2 Heat the oil and butter in a frying pan over medium heat. Add the onion and cook, stirring occasionally, for 15 minutes until onion caramelises.
3 Meanwhile, cook the sweet potato in a medium saucepan of boiling water for 5 minutes or until tender. Drain well.
4 Preheat oven to 400°F/200°C. Prick the pastry lightly with a fork, then line with baking paper. Half-fill with rice and bake for 10 minutes or until lightly browned. Remove the rice and paper. Reduce oven temperature to 350°F/180°C.
5 Cover pastry bases with caramelised onion and top with sweet potato. Whisk together the cream, eggs and basil in a jug, then pour into pastry bases. Bake for 15 minutes or until golden and set.

makes 12

Leek & sun-dried tomato quiches

olive oil spray
1 tablespoon olive oil
1 leek, white part only, halved lengthwise and sliced
4 eggs, lightly beaten
½ cup cream
2 tablespoons milk
¼ cup flat-leaf parsley, freshly chopped
freshly ground black pepper
3 sheets puff pastry, thawed
6–8 sun-dried tomatoes, thinly sliced
2 oz/60 g Danish feta cheese, crumbled

1 Preheat oven to 400°F/200°C. Lightly grease 2 x 12 tart or patty cases with olive oil spray. Heat olive oil in a fry pan.
2 Cook leeks for 2–3 minutes or until soft. Combine eggs, cream, milk, parsley and pepper in a jug.
3 Cut pastry into 3 in/7.5 cm rounds and line tart cases with pastry. Divide leek, sun-dried tomatoes and feta evenly between pastry cases. Pour over egg mixture. Bake for 20–25 minutes or until puffed and golden.

makes about 24

Mini salmon quiches

12 oz/340 g prepared wholemeal shortcrust pastry
1 tablespoon butter
1 onion, finely chopped
8 oz/250 g canned salmon, drained and flaked
2 eggs, lightly beaten
¾ cup milk
¼ teaspoon ground nutmeg
¼ cup fresh dill, chopped
freshly ground black pepper
2 oz/60 g mature Cheddar cheese, grated
¼ bunch fresh chives, snipped

1 Preheat oven to 400°F/200°C.
2 Roll out pastry on a lightly floured surface and use to line six lightly greased 4 in/10 cm flan tins.
3 Melt butter in a frying pan and cook onion for 4–5 minutes, or until soft. Divide onion mixture between flans and spread over pastry. Top with salmon.
4 Place eggs, milk, nutmeg, dill and black pepper to taste in a bowl and mix to combine. Divide egg mixture between flans, sprinkle with cheese and chives and bake for 20 minutes, or until filling is firm.

serves 6

Mini sun-dried tomato quiches

Pastry
2 cups all-purpose (plain) flour, sifted
pinch salt
7 oz/200 g cold butter, cubed
⅓ cup iced water

Filling
3 eggs
1¼ cup cream
salt and freshly ground black pepper
1 cup sun-dried tomatoes, chopped
¼ cup chopped fresh basil

1 Preheat oven to 380°F/190°C. To make the pastry, combine flour, salt and butter in a processor. Process until mixture resembles coarse crumbs. With machine running, add as much iced water as needed to form a ball on top of the blades. Remove to a lightly floured surface, shape ball into a flatter round. Wrap in plastic wrap, refrigerate 1 hour.

2 On a lightly floured surface roll out the dough to ⅛ in/5mm thickness, and use to line about 40 buttered tartlet tins placed on a baking tray. Prick the base lightly with a fork then line with baking paper. Half-fill with rice and blind bake for 10 minutes. Remove the rice and paper and bake for a further five minutes, or until pastry is light brown and set aside to cool.

3 In a bowl, combine eggs with cream and basil. Beat with and electric mixer until well combined and smooth. Season to taste with salt and freshly ground black pepper.

4 Evenly divide the sun-dried tomatoes between each tartlet shell. Pour a little egg mixture on top and bake in an oven until custard has set, about 8 minutes. Remove from oven and let cool slightly before serving.

makes about 40

Quiche Lorraine

Shortcrust pastry
8 oz/250 g plain flour
1 pinch salt
7 oz/200 g very cold butter, cut in cubes

Filling
4 rashers bacon, cut into strips 1 in/2.5 cm
  wide

2 tablespoons onion, finely chopped
2 tablespoons butter
4 eggs
1¾ cups cream
salt and freshly ground black pepper
nutmeg
⅓ cup mature Cheddar, grated
1 tablespoon butter, cubed

1 Preheat oven to 400°F/200°C. To make the pastry, sift the flour and place in a cool bowl. Stir in the salt. Add the butter and rub lightly into the flour with the finger tips until the mixture resembles coarse breadcrumbs. Add 1 tablespoon iced water and mix the crumbs together quickly. Add additional water if necessary to get a compact, slightly damp but not sticky mass. Roll into a ball, wrap in plastic film and place in the refrigerator to rest for at least 15 minutes before use.

2 Line 10 in/25 cm lightly greased flan dish with pastry, line with baking paper and half-fill with rice. Bake in oven 10 minutes, remove paper and rice, return flan dish to oven for 4 minutes until pastry dries and becomes very pale golden. Remove and set aside.

3 Melt butter in frying pan, add onion and sauté until golden. Add bacon and cook 3 minutes, until bacon is soft. Spread the bacon mix on the base of the pastry flan.In bowl, beat eggs, add cream, mix well, add cheese, season to taste with salt, pepper and nutmeg. Gently pour over bacon strips, dot with butter.

4 Place flan dish on baking tray and bake in oven 25 minutes or until top is golden and custard has set. Remove from oven and cool very slightly before serving.

serves 6

Roasted red pepper quiches

16 oz/500 g prepared or ready-rolled shortcrust pastry, thawed
3 tablespoons grated Parmesan cheese

Filling
1 tablespoon butter
1 onion, finely sliced
1 red bell pepper (capsicum), roasted and skin removed
2 eggs
⅔ cup thickened cream
freshly ground black pepper
2 tomatoes, peeled, seeded and chopped
¼ cup fresh basil, finely chopped

1 Preheat oven to 400°F/200°C. Line six lightly greased individual flan dishes with pastry. Line with baking paper and half-fill with rice and bake for 10 minutes. Remove rice and paper, reduce temperature to 350°F/180°C and bake for 10–15 minutes, or until pastry is lightly browned. Set aside to cool.
2 To make filling, melt butter in a small frying pan and cook onion over a medium heat for 5–6 minutes or until soft. Cut capsicum into ½ in/12 mm squares. Place eggs and cream in a bowl and whisk to combine. Season to taste with pepper.
3 Divide onion, tomatoes, basil and capsicum between the pastry shells. Spoon over egg mixture and sprinkle with Parmesan cheese. Bake at 350°F/180°C for 15–20 minutes or until firm.

serves 6

Smoked salmon mini quiches

2 sheets ready-rolled puff pastry
4 oz/125 g smoked salmon, chopped
1 cup thickened cream
3 eggs, lightly beaten
zest of ½ lemon, finely grated
pinch ground nutmeg
¼ bunch dill, chopped
freshly ground black pepper

1 Preheat oven to 350°F/180°C. Cut circles from pastry using a fluted 2 in/5 cm cutter
  and press into shallow patty pans.
2 Divide smoked salmon between pastry cases. Combine cream, eggs, lemon zest,
  nutmeg, dill and pepper, spoon over salmon (pastry cases should only be ⅔ full).
3 Bake in hot oven for 10 minutes or until puffed and golden brown.

makes about 24

Summer vegetable quiche

3 eggplants, cut into ½ in/12 mm cubes
¼ cup olive oil
1 large onion, chopped
2 tomatoes, peeled and chopped
6 eggs
¼ cup milk
2 oz/60 g grated Parmesan cheese
¼ cup breadcrumbs, made from stale bread
¼ bunch fresh chives, snipped
3 tablespoons mature Cheddar cheese, grated

1 Preheat oven to 350°F/180°C. Place eggplants in a colander set over a bowl, sprinkle with salt and set aside to drain for 20 minutes. Wash and pat dry using absorbent kitchen paper.
2 Heat 1 tablespoon oil in a large frying pan and cook onion for 3–4 minutes. Add remaining oil, eggplant and zucchini and cook, stirring frequently, for 5 minutes longer. Stir in tomatoes and simmer, stirring occasionally for 20 minutes, or until mixture is reduced and thickened.
3 Place eggs and milk in a large mixing bowl and whisk to combine. Stir in Parmesan cheese, breadcrumbs and chives. Stir egg mixture into vegetable mixture and spoon into a lightly greased 9 in/23 cm ovenproof dish. Sprinkle with Cheddar and bake for 30 minutes or until set.

serves 6

French onion flans

8 oz/250 g prepared puff pastry
6 oz/170 g mature Cheddar cheese, grated

Onion filling
2 oz/60 g butter
6 onions, sliced
3 eggs
1¾ cups sour cream or natural yoghurt
1 teaspoon ground nutmeg
1½ teaspoon horseradish relish

1 Preheat oven to 400°F/200°C. Roll out pastry and use to line six lightly greased
   4 in/10 cm flan tins.
2 To make filling, melt butter in a frying pan and cook onions over a low heat for 10–15
   minutes or until golden. Divide into six portions and spread over base of flans.
3 Place eggs, sour cream or yoghurt, nutmeg and horseradish in a bowl and mix to
   combine. Pour egg mixture into flans and sprinkle with grated cheese. Bake for
   20 minutes or until flans are set.

serves 6

Vegetable flan

7 oz/200 g prepared shortcrust pastry
2 tablespoons butter
1 tablespoon all-purpose (plain) flour
1¼ cups milk
11 oz/315 g canned sweetcorn kernels, drained
4 oz/125 g peas, cooked
4 scallions (spring onions), chopped
freshly ground black pepper
2 eggs
4 oz/125 g mature Cheddar cheese, grated

1 Preheat oven to 350°F/180°C.
2 Roll out pastry to fit a 9 in/23 cm flan tin. Prick pastry case with fork, line with baking paper and half-fill with uncooked rice. Bake for 8 minutes, then remove rice and paper and bake for 10 minutes longer or until pastry is golden.
3 Melt butter in a saucepan and cook flour for 1 minute. Gradually stir in milk and cook over a medium heat, stirring constantly for 4–5 minutes or until mixture boils and thickens. Add corn, peas, spring onion and black pepper to taste, then mix in eggs.
4 Pour corn mixture into pastry case, sprinkle with cheese and bake for 30 minutes or until set and golden.

serves 4

Blue cheese flans

13 oz/370 g prepared or ready-rolled
 puff pastry, thawed
2 tablespoons butter
2 onions, finely sliced

Filling
6 eggs
1 cup cream
1⅓ cups milk

freshly ground black pepper
7 oz/200 g blue cheese, crumbled

Cranberry sauce
1 cup cranberry sauce
½ cup Port or red wine
½ teaspoon ground allspice
2 teaspoons cornflour, blended with
 4 tablespoons water

1 Preheat oven to 400°F/200°C. Line ten greased 5 in/12 cm individual flan tins with pastry. Melt butter in a small frying pan and cook onions for 10 minutes or until soft and golden. Divide evenly and spread over base of flans.
2 To make filling, place eggs, cream and pepper in a bowl and mix to combine. Stir in cheese, spoon mixture into flans and bake for 25–30 minutes or until firm and golden.
3 To make sauce, place cranberry sauce, port and allspice in a saucepan, bring to the boil, then reduce heat and simmer for 5 minutes. Stir in cornflour mixture and cook until sauce thickens. Serve with hot or warm flans.

serves 10

Turkey & asparagus quiche

¾ cup cooked, diced turkey
10 oz/300 g canned asparagus cuts, drained
4 eggs, beaten
1 tablespoon flour
1 cup sour cream
1 cup milk
salt and freshly ground black pepper to taste

1 Line a deep 8 in/20 cm quiche flan and refrigerate for 30 minutes. Line the pastry with a sheet of baking paper and half-fill with rice. Bake in the oven 400°F/200°C for 10 minutes. Remove paper and rice and bake for a further 10 minutes. Reduce oven to 350°F/180°C.
2 Combine the eggs, flour, sour cream, milk, salt and pepper.
3 Place asparagus and turkey on the base of the flan. Pour combined ingredients over the asparagus and turkey. Bake for 25–30 minutes until set. Serve either hot or cold.

serves 6

Tuna quiche

½ quantity rich shortcrust pastry
½ cup cream cheese
7 oz/200 g canned tuna, drained
4 eggs, beaten
1 tablespoon flour
juice of ½ lemon
1½ cups cream
½ cup milk
salt and freshly ground black pepper to taste
4 rashers bacon, chopped
⅓ cup tasty cheese

1 Preheat oven to 350°F/180°C. Line a deep 8 in/20 cm quiche flan. Refrigerate for 30 minutes. Line the pastry with a sheet of baking paper and half-fill with rice. Bake for 10 minutes. Remove loading and bake for a further 10 minutes.
2 Combine the cream cheese and tuna and beat well. To this mixture add the eggs, flour, lemon juice, cream, milk, salt and pepper.
3 Sauté bacon over a medium heat. Drain well. Place bacon and cheese on the base of the flan. Pour combined ingredients over the bacon and cheese. Bake for 25–30 minutes until set. Serve either hot or cold.

serves 6

Spinach & bacon quiche

½ quantity rich shortcrust pastry
1 bunch spinach, purée
4 eggs
1 tablespoon plain flour
¼ teaspoon basil
1½ cups cream
½ cup milk
salt and freshly ground black pepper to taste
4 rashers bacon, medium diced
⅔ cup grated Cheddar cheese

1 Preheat oven to 350°F/180°C. Line a deep 8 in/20 cm quiche flan. Refrigerate for
   30 minutes. Line the pastry with a sheet of baking paper and half-fill with rice. Bake for
   10 minutes. Remove paper and rice and bake for a further 10 minutes at 350°F/180°C.
2 Beat the spinach purée, eggs, flour, basil, cream, milk, salt and pepper together.
3 Sauté bacon over a medium heat. Drain well. Place bacon and cheese on the base
   of the flan. Pour combined ingredients over the bacon and cheese. Bake for 25–30
   minutes until set. Serve either hot or cold.

serves 8

Herbed tomato cheese quiche

½ quantity rich shortcrust pastry
4 rashers bacon, medium diced
⅔ cup grated Cheddar cheese
4 eggs
1 tablespoon all-purpose (plain) flour
¼ teaspoon thyme
1½ cups cream
½ cup milk
salt and freshly ground black pepper to taste
1 large tomato, sliced

1 Preheat oven to 350°F/180°C. Line a deep 8 in/20 cm quiche flan. Refrigerate for 30 minutes. Line the pastry with a sheet of baking paper and half-fill with rice. Bake in the oven for 10 minutes. Remove rice and paper and bake for a further 10 minutes.
2 Beat eggs, flour, thyme, cream, milk, salt and pepper well together.
3 Sauté bacon over a medium heat. Drain well. Place bacon and cheese on the base of the flan. Pour combined ingredients over the bacon and cheese and layer tomatoes on top. Bake in the oven for 25–30 minutes until set. Serve either hot or cold.

serves 8

Seafood quiche

2 x 8 oz/250 g cans red salmon
1 cup mayonnaise
1¼ cups sour cream
14 oz/400 g can cream of oyster soup
¼ bunch dill, chopped
¼ bunch chives, chopped
few drops Tabasco sauce
zest of ½ lemon
1 cup shrimp (prawns), shelled
5 teaspoons gelatine
9 in/23 cm shortcrust pastry case

1 Place the undrained salmon into a bowl and break up lightly with a fork, removing bones.
2 Stir in the mayonnaise, sour cream, oyster soup, dill, chives, Tabasco sauce, lemon zest and prawns, reserving a few for decoration.
3 Add the gelatine to ½ cup of hot water and stir briskly with a fork until dissolved. Stir into the salmon mixture.
4 Spoon into the chilled pastry case and refrigerate until firm.
5 Serve in slices with accompanying salads.

serves 4

Danish flan

2 thick slices ham
1 chicken breast, cooked and skinned
6 gherkins
½ teaspoon mustard
pinch pepper
pinch nutmeg
4 teaspoons gelatine
½ cup cream
3 egg whites
1 shortcrust flan case 8 in/20 cm

1 Chop the ham and chicken finely. Chop the gherkins and add to the meat, with the mustard, pepper and nutmeg. Add the gelatine to ¼ cup of hot water and stir briskly with a fork until dissolved. Cool slightly then add to the ham mixture.
2 Whip the cream lightly and fold into mixture. Refrigerate until just beginning to thicken. Whisk the egg whites until soft peaks form. Fold into thickening mixture.
3 Pile into cold prepared flan case and refrigerate until set firm.

serves 4

Frittatas

Potato & carrot frittata

¼ cup finely chopped onions
4 tablespoons butter
1 cup potatoes, cooked and cut into 12 mm/½ in cubes
½ cup cooked and sliced carrots
1 tablespoon oil
1 tablespoon chopped fresh basil
3 tablespoons Parmesan cheese, grated
5 eggs
½ cup cream
salt
pepper

1 Sauté onion in 1 tablespoon butter for 5 minutes, until golden. Add 1 more tablespoon butter to frying pan, add oil, potatoes and carrots. Sauté over medium high heat until potatoes brown. Remove mixture from frying pan, mix in basil and Parmesan.
2 Combine eggs, cream, salt and pepper, mix into potato and carrot mixture.
3 Add remaining butter to frying pan, melt and add egg mixture. Cook over low heat till bottom has browned. Slide onto plate, return to pan and cook other side. Serve warm.

serves 4

Spinach frittata

2 tablespoons olive oil
2 cloves garlic, crushed
1 bunch (about 12 leaves) spinach, chopped
6 eggs
¼ cup cream
¼ teaspoon ground nutmeg
freshly ground black pepper
¾ cup grated Emmental cheese

1 Heat oil in a frying pan, add garlic and spinach, stir over heat until spinach releases water, and until water has evaporated. Cool.
2 Lightly beat eggs, add cream, nutmeg, pepper and cheese. Stir in spinach.
3 Pour into a greased 23 cm/9 in flan dish. Bake in moderate oven for 20 minutes or until set.

serves 4

Vegetable frittata

3 tablespoons olive oil
1 onion, sliced
10 asparagus spears, trimmed and cut into 2.5 cm pieces
2 zucchini, cut into thin strips
1 red bell pepper (capsicum), cut into thin strips
8 eggs, lightly beaten
4 tablespoons grated Parmesan cheese
3 tablespoons sour cream or natural yoghurt
freshly ground black pepper

1 Heat oil in a large frying pan and cook onion, asparagus, zucchini and red bell pepper over a medium heat for 3–4 minutes or until vegetables just start to soften.
2 Place eggs, Parmesan cheese, sour cream or yoghurt and black pepper to taste in a bowl and beat to combine. Pour egg mixture over vegetables in pan, reduce heat to low and cook for 10 minutes or until frittata is almost set.
3 Place frying pan under a preheated medium grill and cook frittata for 2–3 minutes or until top is set. Serve cut into wedges.

serves 4

Avocado & feta frittata

2 avocados, cut into 2.5 cm/1 in pieces
2 teaspoons lemon juice
1 teaspoon salt
4 oz/125 g feta cheese, crumbled
16 black olives, stoned and sliced
1 teaspoon fresh rosemary leaves, chopped
12 eggs
1 teaspoon freshly ground black pepper
1 tablespoon olive oil

1 Combine avocado pieces in a bowl with lemon juice and salt. Add feta cheese, olives
   and rosemary, combine gently.
2 Beat eggs with freshly ground black pepper and a little salt. Heat oil in a heavy frying
   pan over moderate heat. Add eggs and cook until bottom is set.
3 Spread avocado mixture on top, take off the heat and finish cooking under a hot grill,
   until the top has set and the edges start to brown. To serve, cut into wedges.

makes 12 wedges

Coconut cream frittata

4 oz/125 g dried yellow mung beans,
  soaked in water overnight
2 eggs
2 tablespoons vegetable oil
1 onion, sliced
2 potatoes, peeled and grated
2 carrots, grated
2 zucchini, grated
4 oz/125 g can corn kernels, drained

3 tablespoons chopped fresh basil
freshly ground black pepper
4 oz/125 g grated tasty cheese

Coconut cream
½ cup coconut cream
1 tablespoon lemon juice
2 tablespoons chopped fresh mint

1 Drain mung beans and place in food processor or blender with eggs and process until smooth. Place mung bean mixture in a large mixing bowl.
2 Heat one tablespoon oil in a frying pan and cook onion gently for 3–4 minutes. Add potatoes, carrots and zucchini and cook, stirring for 5 minutes or until vegetables soften. Remove from pan and pat dry with absorbent kitchen paper. Combine cooked vegetables, bean mixture, corn kernels and basil. Mix and season to taste with pepper.
3 Heat remaining oil in a large frying pan, add vegetable mixture and sprinkle with cheese. Cook over a low heat for 5–8 minutes or until just firm, shaking pan occasionally to ensure that the frittata does not stick. Place pan under a preheated grill for 3 minutes, or until the frittata is browned on the top.
4 To make cream, place coconut cream, lemon juice and mint in a screw-top jar and shake well to combine. Invert frittata onto a plate, cut into wedges and serve with coconut cream.

serves 6

Summer frittata

2 tablespoons margarine
1 clove garlic, crushed
4 zucchini, sliced
8 eggs, lightly beaten
2 tablespoons chopped sun-dried tomatoes
6 scallions (spring onions), finely chopped
1 tablespoon chopped fresh basil
1 tablespoon chopped fresh mint
freshly ground black pepper
2 tablespoons grated tasty cheese

1 Melt margarine in a large frying pan and cook garlic and zucchini over a medium heat for 5–6 minutes, or until zucchini are just tender.
2 Place eggs, tomatoes, spring onions, basil and mint in a bowl and mix to combine. Season to taste with pepper. Pour over zucchini in pan and gently move vegetables to allow the egg mixture to run under. Reduce heat to low and cook until frittata is brown on the base and just set.
3 Slide onto an oven tray, sprinkle with cheese and place under a preheated grill for 4–5 minutes or until cheese melts and is golden. Serve hot, warm or at room temperature, cut into wedges.

serves 6

Asparagus & herb frittata

1 lb/500 g fresh asparagus, trimmed to 6 in/15 cm lengths
12 medium eggs
2 small cloves garlic, crushed
1 cup mixed herbs, including basil, chives and parsley, chopped
salt and freshly ground black pepper
2 oz/60 g butter
3½ oz/100 g ricotta
squeeze of lemon juice
olive oil or truffle oil, to drizzle
Parmesan, to serve
fresh chives, to garnish

1 Preheat the grill to high. Place the asparagus in a grill pan and grill for 10 minutes or until charred and tender, turning once. Keep warm.
2 Meanwhile, whisk together the eggs, garlic, herbs and seasoning. Melt 1 oz/30 g of the butter in an ovenproof frying pan until it starts to foam, then immediately pour in a quarter of the egg mixture and cook for 1–2 minutes, stirring occasionally, until almost set.
3 Place under the preheated grill for 3–4 minutes, until the egg is cooked through and the top of the frittata is set, then transfer to a plate. Keep warm while you make the 3 remaining frittatas, adding more butter when necessary.
4 Arrange a quarter of the asparagus and a quarter of the ricotta over each frittata, squeeze over the lemon juice, season and drizzle with oil. Top with shavings of Parmesan and garnish with fresh chives.

serves 4

Bean frittata

1 teaspoon vegetable oil
½ tomato, chopped
3 oz/90 g canned three-bean mix
2 eggs, lightly beaten
¼ cup milk
1 oz/30 g mature Cheddar cheese, grated

1 Heat oil in a small frying pan over a medium heat, add tomato and cook for 1 minute or until soft. Add beans and mix to combine.
2 Place eggs, milk and cheese in a bowl and whisk to combine. Pour egg mixture over bean mixture in pan and cook over a low heat, without stirring, for 5 minutes or until frittata is firm.

serves 2

Cheesy potato frittata

1 potato, cooked and cooled
2 rashers bacon
4 eggs
freshly ground black pepper
2 tablespoons butter
1 oz/30 g mature Cheddar cheese, grated

1 Cut potato into ½ in/12 mm cubes. Set aside. Cut rind from bacon, then cut bacon into strips. Set aside. Break eggs into bowl. Add black pepper to taste. Whisk, then set aside.
2 Place butter in frying pan. Heat over a medium heat until butter melts and sizzles. Add bacon and cook, stirring, for 2–3 minutes or until cooked. Add potato to pan. Cook, stirring, for 5 minutes or until potato is brown. Pour egg mixture into pan. Turn heat to low. Cook for 10 minutes or until frittata is almost set.
3 Preheat grill to high. Sprinkle top of frittata with cheese. Place pan under grill. Cook for 2–3 minutes or until cheese melts. Cut frittata into wedges to serve.

serves 4

Ham, potato & vegetable frittata

1 potato, cooked and cooled
2 rashers bacon
4 eggs
freshly ground black pepper
2 tablespoons butter
1 oz/30 g mature Cheddar cheese, grated

1 Cut potato into ½ in/12 mm cubes. Set aside. Cut rind from bacon, then cut bacon
  into strips. Set aside. Break eggs into bowl. Add black pepper to taste. Whisk, then
  set aside.
2 Place butter in frying pan. Heat over a medium heat until butter melts and sizzles. Add
  bacon and cook, stirring, for 2–3 minutes or until cooked. Add potato to pan. Cook,
  stirring, for 5 minutes or until potato is brown. Pour egg mixture into pan. Turn heat to
  low. Cook for 10 minutes or until frittata is almost set.
3 Preheat grill to high. Sprinkle top of frittata with cheese. Place pan under grill. Cook
  for 2–3 minutes or until cheese melts. Cut frittata into wedges to serve.

serves 4

Individual frittata

1 tablespoon butter
1 onion, chopped
1 clove garlic, crushed
2 slices ham, chopped
½ fresh red chilli, finely chopped
1 red bell pepper (capsicum), finely chopped
2 scallions (spring onions), chopped
4 oz/125 g canned pineapple pieces, drained
½ cup fresh parsley, finely chopped
4 eggs
¾ cup milk
1 oz/30 g mature Cheddar cheese, grated

1 Preheat oven to 350°F/180°C. Melt butter in a large frying pan and cook onion, garlic, ham, chilli, red capsicum and spring onions over a medium heat for 3–4 minutes or until onion is soft. Stir in pineapple pieces and parsley, remove pan from heat and set aside to cool for 10 minutes.
2 Place eggs, milk and cheese in a bowl and mix to combine. Stir in ham mixture. Divide mixture between four 4 in/10 cm lightly greased flan tins and bake for 20–25 minutes or until set.

serves 4

Peppers and potato frittata

2 potatoes
1 zucchini (courgette)
2 roasted bell peppers (red capsicums)
4 eggs
salt
freshly ground black pepper
3 tablespoons oil

1   Peel and grate potatoes. Trim and grate zucchini. Cut capsicums into thin strips. Lightly beat eggs. Season with salt and pepper. Mix in potatoes, zucchini and capsicums.
2   Heat oil in a large frying pan. Pour in egg mixture. Cook over a medium heat for about 8 minutes or until egg is set. Cut in half and turn to cook other side until golden. To serve, cut into small wedges. Serve warm or cold.

makes 16 wedges

Ham, cheese & pea frittata

2 tablespoons olive oil
1 red onion, thinly sliced
9 eggs
8 oz/250 g leg ham, cut into ½ in/12 mm cubes
1 cup peas
2 cups cooked short pasta
1 cup Cheddar cheese, grated
pickles, to serve

1 Heat oil in a 9 in/22 cm ovenproof frypan over medium heat. Cook onion, stirring, for 2–3 minutes until softened but not coloured.
2 Meanwhile, whisk eggs in a bowl with salt and pepper. Add ham, peas, pasta and cheese to the pan with the onion.
3 Pour the whisked eggs over the pan ingredients, then reduce heat to very low and cook for 6–8 minutes until almost firm, tilting the pan and drawing in the sides from time to time so egg cooks evenly.
4 Preheat the grill to medium, then place pan under the grill for 3–4 minutes until top is golden. Cool slightly, then turn out and slice. Serve with pickles and salad.

serves 4

Tarts and Pies

Baby spinach tarts

Pastry
1½ cups plain flour
4 tablespoons grated Parmesan cheese
4 oz/125 g butter, chopped

Spinach filling
2 teaspoons olive oil
2 scallions (spring onions), chopped

1 clove garlic, crushed
8 spinach leaves, shredded
4 oz/125 g ricotta cheese, drained
2 eggs, lightly beaten
⅓ cup milk
½ teaspoon grated nutmeg
4 tablespoons pine nuts

1 Preheat oven to 400°F/200°C. To make pastry, place flour, Parmesan cheese and butter in a food processor and process until mixture resembles fine breadcrumbs.
2 With machine running, slowly add 2–3 tablespoons of iced water to form a soft dough. Turn dough onto a lightly floured surface and knead briefly. Wrap dough in cling wrap and refrigerate for 30 minutes.
3 Roll out pastry to 1/10 in/3 mm thick. Using an 3 in/8 cm fluted pastry cutter, cut out twenty pastry rounds. Place pastry rounds in lightly greased patty tins. Pierce base and sides of pastry with a fork and bake for 5–10 minutes or until lightly golden. Reduce oven temperature to 350°F/180°C.
4 To make filling, heat oil in a frying pan over a medium heat. Add spring onions, garlic and spinach and cook, stirring, until spinach is wilted. Remove pan from heat and set aside to cool.
5 Place spinach mixture, ricotta cheese, eggs, milk and nutmeg in a bowl and mix to combine. Spoon filling into pastry cases, sprinkle with pine nuts and bake for 15–20 minutes or until tarts are golden and filling is set.

makes 20

Italian spinach tart

2 cups all-purpose (plain) flour
pinch of salt
4 oz/125 g butter
1 lb/500 g spinach
7 oz/200 g ricotta cheese
4 eggs, beaten
2 oz/60 g Parmesan cheese, grated
grated nutmeg
salt and freshly ground black pepper

1 Sift the flour and salt into a large bowl. Cut the butter into small pieces, add it to the flour. Rub the butter into the flour with your fingertips until the mixture resembles breadcrumbs. Don't overdo this as the butter will be blended more thoroughly later.
2 Make a well in the centre. Mix in ¼ cup iced water and combine quickly with a knife. Press the dough together with your fingers.
3 Turn out onto a floured board and knead lightly until smooth. Roll into a ball and brush off excess flour. Wrap in cling wrap and refrigerate for 20–30 minutes.
4 Preheat oven to 400°F/200°C. Roll out the pastry and use it to line a 10 in/25 cm flan ring. Trim the edges. Prick the base lightly with a fork and line with baking paper. Half-fill with dried beans and bake 'blind' for 7 minutes. Remove the beans and paper and bake for a further 5 minutes. Reduce oven temperature to 350°F/180°C.
5 Meanwhile, wash the spinach and place it in a saucepan with the water clinging to the leaves. Cover and cook until tender, then drain, squeeze dry, cool and chop finely. In a bowl, beat the ricotta until smooth, then beat in the eggs, Parmesan, nutmeg and spinach. Season the mixture and pour it into the prebaked pastry shell. Bake for 25–30 minutes until golden and set. Serve cold.

serves 4

Leek & dill tart

10 oz/300 g prepared shortcrust pastry

Leek filling
1 tablespoon butter
4 leeks, trimmed and thinly sliced
1 cup natural yoghurt
1 tablespoon plain flour
2 eggs, lightly beaten
3 oz/90 g Cheddar cheese, grated
½ bunch fresh dill, chopped
freshly ground black pepper

1 Preheat oven to 400°F/200°C. Roll out pastry to line a lightly greased 8 in/20 cm loose-bottom flan tin. Prick base several times with a fork, line with baking paper and half-fill with uncooked rice. Bake for 8–10 minutes, remove rice and paper and bake for a further 5 minutes, until pastry is golden. Set aside to cool.
2 To make the filling, melt butter in a frying pan and cook leeks for 4–5 minutes or until just tender. Place yoghurt, flour, eggs, three quarters of the cheese and 1 tablespoon of dill in a bowl and mix to combine. Fold in leeks, season to taste with black pepper and spoon into pastry case.
3 Sprinkle tart with remaining cheese and dill and bake for 20 minutes or until tart is set.

serves 4

Smoked salmon & asparagus pies

2 asparagus spears
3½ oz/100 g smoked salmon, chopped
1 sprig dill, leaves removed and chopped
2 scallions (spring onions), sliced
1 egg, lightly beaten
1 large sheet shortcrust pastry

1 Snap the pale bottom ends from the asparagus and discard. Chop asparagus spears, then blanch in boiling water for 2 minutes. Drain, then combine with salmon, dill, spring onions and egg.
2 Preheat the oven to 400°F/200°C. Using a pastry cutter 5 in/12 cm in diameter, cut 4 rounds out of the pastry. Cut five 1 in/2.5 cm-long incisions evenly around the edge of the pastry rounds.
3 Place the pastry rounds into large muffin tin moulds, making sure that the pastry slightly overlaps where the incisions have been made. Divide filling evenly between each pie case and bake for 15–20 minutes.

serves 4

Orange chocolate tarts

13 oz/370 g prepared shortcrust pastry
4 oz/125 g dark chocolate, melted

Orange filling
3 egg yolks
2 tablespoons sugar
1¼ cups milk, scalded
zest of ½ orange, finely grated
2 tablespoons Grand Marnier (orange liqueur)
1½ teaspoons gelatine, dissolved in 4 teaspoons hot water, cooled
¼ cup double cream, whipped

1 Preheat oven to 400°F/200°C. Roll pastry out and line six 4 in/10 cm flan tins. Line pastry cases with baking paper and half-fill with uncooked rice. Bake for 8 minutes, then remove rice and paper and bake for 10 minutes longer or until pastry is golden. Set aside to cool completely. Brush cooled pastry cases with melted chocolate and set aside until chocolate sets.
2 To make filling, place egg yolks and sugar in a heatproof bowl over a saucepan of simmering water, beating until a ribbon trail forms when beater is lifted from mixture. Remove bowl from heat and gradually whisk in milk. Transfer mixture to a heavy-based saucepan and cook over a low heat, stirring in a figure eight pattern, until mixture thickens and coats the back of a wooden spoon. Do not allow the mixture to boil. Remove from heat, place in a pan of ice and stir until cool.
3 Stir in orange zest, Grand Marnier and gelatine mixture. Fold in cream, then spoon filling into pastry cases. Refrigerate until set.

serves 6

Chicken & leek pie

1 quantity basic shortcrust pastry (see page 233)
2 medium leeks, washed and sliced
2 oz/60 g butter
1 tablespoon oil
13 oz/375 g chicken flesh, chopped finely
3 leaves sage, finely chopped
salt and freshly ground black pepper to taste
¾ cup Gruyère cheese, grated
⅔ cup cream
2 eggs

1 Preheat oven to 400°F/200°C. Roll out pastry and line a 9 in/23 cm pie plate. Prick the bottom of the pastry shell with a fork and refrigerate the shell for 1 hour. Line the shell with baking paper and half-fill with rice. Bake for 10 minutes. Remove paper and rice and bake the shell for a further 10–15 minutes or until it is lightly coloured. Allow to cool. Reduce oven heat to 350°F/180°C.
2 In a saucepan, over a low heat, sauté the leeks in butter and oil for 15 minutes or until the leeks are soft. Add the chicken meat and cook for a further 5 minutes.
3 Stir in sage and seasonings. Allow mixture to cool. Beat the cream and egg together. Sprinkle ½ cup cheese on base of shell, add the chicken mixture and pour over egg mixture. Sprinkle with remaining cheese and bake for 35 minutes. Cut into slices and serve.

serves 6–8

Tomato egg pie

Shortcrust pastry
8 oz/250 g plain flour
1 pinch salt
7 oz/200 g very cold butter, cut in cubes

Filling
4 tomatoes, sliced

salt and freshly ground black pepper
¼ cup fresh basil, chopped
3 eggs
½ cup cream
¼ cup yoghurt
2 tablespoons Parmesan cheese, grated
1 tablespoon butter, cubed, extra

1 Preheat oven to 350°F/180°C. To make the pastry, sift the flour and place in a cool bowl. Stir in the salt. Add the butter and rub lightly into the flour with the finger-tips until the mixture resembles coarse breadcrumbs.

2 Add one tablespoon iced water and mix the crumbs together quickly. Add a little more iced water if necessary to get a compact, slightly damp but not sticky mass. Roll into a ball, wrap in cling wrap and place in the refrigerator to rest for at least 15 minutes before use.

3 Roll out pastry to line a 10 in/25 cm flan tin. Prick pastry case with fork, line with baking paper and half-fill with uncooked rice. Bake for 8 minutes, then remove rice or beans and paper and bake for 10 minutes longer or until pastry is golden.

4 Arrange tomatoes in one layer in pastry shell. Season with salt and pepper to taste, sprinkle on basil. Combine eggs with cream and yoghurt, pour gently over tomatoes, sprinkle on Parmesan cheese, dot with butter and bake in oven for 25 minutes or until top is golden and eggs have set. Let cool slightly and serve.

serves 6

Leek & apple pie

13 oz/370 g prepared shortcrust pastry

Apple and leek filling
1 tablespoon butter
1 cooking apple, cored, peeled and sliced
3 small leeks, sliced
4 rashers bacon, chopped
¼ teaspoon ground cloves
¼ teaspoon ground nutmeg
2 oz/60 g blue cheese, crumbled
3 eggs, lightly beaten
¾ cup double cream
2 tablespoons Port
freshly ground black pepper

1 Preheat oven to 430°F/220°C. To make filling, melt butter in a frying pan and cook apple, leeks and bacon over a medium heat for 5–8 minutes or until apple softens. Add cloves and nutmeg and cook for 1 minute longer. Set aside to cool.
2 Roll our pastry on a lightly floured surface and line the base and sides of a lightly greased 9 in/23 cm flan tin. Prick base of pastry with a fork, line with baking paper and half-fill with uncooked rice. Bake for 10 minutes. Remove rice and paper. Reduce oven temperature to 350°F/180°C.
3 Spread apple mixture over base of pastry case. Place cheese, eggs, cream, Port (if used) and black pepper to taste in a bowl, mix to combine and carefully pour into pastry case. Bake for 30–35 minutes or until pie is firm.

serves 8

Soufflés

Cheese & chives soufflés

2 oz/60 g butter
½ cup all-purpose (plain) flour
1¼ cups hot milk
4 oz/125 g mature Cheddar cheese, grated
1 teaspoon ground nutmeg
3 eggs, separated
½ bunch fresh chives, snipped

1 Preheat oven to 400°F/200°C. Melt butter in a saucepan and cook flour over a medium heat, stirring constantly for 1 minute. Reduce heat, stir in hot milk and whisk over a low heat until sauce is smooth and thickens.
2 Remove pan from heat and set aside to cool for 10 minutes. Stir in cheese, nutmeg, egg yolks and chives.
3 Place egg whites in a bowl and beat until soft peaks form. Fold egg white mixture into sauce. Divide soufflé mixture between six greased and collared ½ cup capacity soufflé dishes and bake for 15–20 minutes or until soufflés are puffed and golden.

serves 6

Corn & chilli soufflé

3 tablespoons breadcrumbs, made form stale bread
2 oz/60 g butter
1 onion, finely chopped
1 red chilli, seeds removed and finely chopped
¼ cup all-purpose (plain) flour
½ cup milk
11 oz/315 g canned creamed sweetcorn
4 egg yolks
freshly ground black pepper
5 egg whites

1 Preheat oven to 400°F/200°C. Grease an 7 in/18 cm soufflé dish, sprinkle with breadcrumbs and set aside.
2 Melt butter in a saucepan and cook onion and chilli over a medium heat for 10 minutes, or until onion is soft and golden. Stir in flour and cook for 1 minute longer. Remove pan from heat and gradually stir in milk and corn. Return to heat and cook, stirring constantly, until mixture boils and thickens. Remove from heat and beat in egg yolks one at a time. Season to taste with black pepper.
3 Place egg whites in a bowl and beat until stiff peaks form. Fold gently into corn mixture.
4 Spoon soufflé mixture into prepared dish and bake for 30–35 minutes or until soufflé is puffed and golden. Serve immediately.

serves 4

Eggplant soufflé

2½ oz/75 g butter
2 cloves garlic, crushed
1 onion, finely chopped
1 large eggplant, peeled and finely chopped
2 cups milk
7 eggs
2 tablespoons plain flour
4 oz/125 g grated mature Cheddar cheese

1 Preheat oven to 350°F/180°C. Melt 3 tablespoons butter in a large frying pan and cook garlic and onion for 2 minutes. Add eggplant and cook for 5 minutes longer. Add ½ cup of water to pan, cover and simmer over a low heat for 1 hour, stirring frequently, adding more water if necessary.
2 Place 1½ cups milk and remaining butter in a saucepan and bring to the boil. Place remaining milk, 5 egg yolks, 2 whole eggs and flour in a bowl and whisk to combine. Slowly whisk egg mixture into boiling milk, reduce heat and cook, whisking constantly, until sauce thickens. Remove pan from heat and stir in eggplant mixture and cheese.
3 Place 5 egg whites in a bowl and beat until stiff peaks form. Fold egg whites into sauce, then spoon into a lightly greased 8 in/20 cm soufflé dish with collar attached. Bake for 35 minutes. Serve immediately.

serves 4

Smoked salmon soufflés

3 tablespoons Parmesan cheese, grated
1 tablespoon butter
2 tablespoons all-purpose (plain) flour
½ cup milk
¼ cup double cream
3 eggs, separated
2 oz/60 g grated Gruyère cheese
2 oz/60 g smoked salmon, shredded
½ bunch fresh dill, chopped

1 Preheat oven to 350°F/180°C. Grease two one-cup capacity ramekins and sprinkle base and sides with 2 tablespoons Parmesan cheese.
2 Melt butter in a small saucepan over a medium heat. Stir in flour and cook for 2 minutes. Remove pan from heat and gradually whisk in milk and cream. Return pan to heat and cook, stirring constantly, for 4 minutes or until sauce boils and thickens. Remove pan from heat and set aside to cool slightly. Add egg yolks, Gruyère cheese, remaining Parmesan cheese, salmon and dill to sauce and mix to combine.
3 Place egg whites in a bowl and beat until stiff peaks form. Fold egg white mixture into salmon mixture. Pour soufflé mixture into ramekins and bake for 20–25 minutes or until soufflés are puffed and golden. Serve immediately.

serves 2

Asparagus soufflé

¼ cup butter
¼ cup all-purpose (plain) flour
1 cup milk
4 eggs, separated
1 cup finely chopped asparagus, cooked, well drained
freshly ground black pepper
sea salt

1 Preheat oven to 380°F/190°C. Over low heat, blend the butter, flour, and milk, to a smooth mixture. Remove from heat, add egg yolks and blend. Stir in asparagus and season to taste. With an electric mixer beat egg whites until stiff and carefully fold into mixture.
2 Bake in a greased 8 pint/2 litre baking dish in the oven for 30–40 minutes, or until puffed up.

serves 4

Passionfruit soufflé

1 tablespoon butter, softened
1 tablespoon superfine (caster) sugar
4 oz/125 g canned passionfruit pulp
⅔ cup confectioners' (icing) sugar
2 egg yolks
1 tablespoon orange juice
6 egg whites

Nectarine cream
2 very ripe nectarines, peeled and stones
  removed
1¼ cups double cream
2 tablespoons icing sugar
2 tablespoons Grand Marnier (orange
  liqueur)

1 Preheat oven to 350°F/180°C. Brush four 1½ cup capacity soufflé dishes with butter, then sprinkle with caster sugar. Turn dishes upside down to allow excess sugar to fall out.

2 Place passionfruit pulp, ½ cup icing sugar, egg yolks and orange juice in a large bowl and mix well to combine. Place egg whites in a mixing bowl and beat until soft peaks form, add remaining icing sugar and beat until just combined. Mix ¼ egg white mixture into the passionfruit mixture, then gently fold in the remaining egg whites. Spoon into prepared soufflé dishes and bake for 8–10 minutes or until well risen and golden.

3 To make nectarine cream, place nectarine flesh in a food processor or blender to purée. Place cream, icing sugar and Grand Marnier (orange liqueur) in a bowl and beat until soft peaks form. Gently fold cream mixture into nectarine purée. Chill until ready to serve.

4 Serve souffles with nectarine cream.

serves 4

Individual kiwifruit soufflés

3 cups water
5 tablespoons sugar
½ teaspoon vanilla extract
13 oz/370 g kiwifruit, peeled and halved
2 egg yolks
7 egg whites
1 tablespoon butter, melted
2 tablespoons caster sugar

1 Preheat oven to 430°F/220°C. Combine sugar and 3 tablespoons of water in saucepan, bring to the boil, reduce to a simmer, add vanilla extract and stir. Add kiwifruit and simmer for 15 minutes. Drain, place in a food processor and process to a purée. Add more sugar to taste and while the motor is running add egg yolks.
2 Beat egg whites until firm, but not too stiff and dry. Mix one fourth into the purée. Fold in remaining egg whites lightly but thoroughly.
3 Brush insides of eight individual 1½ cup soufflé dishes with butter, dust with caster sugar. Shake out excess. Spoon soufflé mixture into dishes. Level top and run your thumb along the inside rim, pushing mixture away from edge; this will help soufflé to rise.
4 Cook in oven for 8 minutes, or until well risen. Serve immediately.

serves 8

Coffee Brazil soufflés

2½ oz/75 g cooking chocolate, grated
3 tablespoons Coffee Brazil liqueur
4 eggs, separated
2½ tablespoons instant coffee
½ cup superfine (caster) sugar
4 cups cream, whipped
1 teaspoon cocoa
1 tablespoon confectioners' (icing) sugar

1 Melt the chocolate in 1 tablespoon of water with Coffee Brazil liqueur over a medium heat. Cool and set to one side.
2 Beat the egg yolks, coffee and sugar together until well combined. Add the cooled chocolate mixture and stir in. Lightly fold the whipped cream into the mix
3 Beat the egg whites until stiff and gently fold into the coffee cream and spoon into individual serving bowls and refrigerate for at least 4 hours before use.
4 Mix cocoa and icing sugar together. Sprinkle over each soufflé before serving.

serves 6

Cheesy herb soufflé

3 tablespoons butter
¼ cup all-purpose (plain) flour
1 cup milk
5 oz/150 g Cheddar cheese, grated
2½ oz/75 g Parmesan cheese, grated
¼ teaspoon ground nutmeg
½ bunch fresh flat-leaf parsley, chopped
½ bunch fresh chives, snipped
1 cup fresh basil, finely chopped
1 cup fresh coriander, chopped
freshly ground black pepper to taste
4 eggs, separated

1 Preheat oven to 400°F/200°C. Melt butter in a large saucepan and cook flour over a medium heat for 1 minute. Gradually stir in milk and cook, stirring constantly, until sauce is thick and smooth.
2 Stir in Cheddar cheese, Parmesan cheese, nutmeg, parsley, chives, basil, coriander and black pepper to taste, then beat in egg yolks one at a time.
3 Place egg whites in a clean bowl and beat until soft peaks form. Fold 2 tablespoons cheese mixture into egg whites, then fold egg white mixture into remaining cheese mixture.
4 Spoon soufflé mixture into a lightly greased 4-cup capacity soufflé dish and bake for 25–30 minutes or until soufflé is fluffed and golden. Serve immediately.

serves 4

Crêpes and Pancakes

Basic crêpes

1 cup all-purpose (plain) flour, sifted
2 eggs
¼ teaspoon salt
1 cup milk
3 tablespoons melted butter

1 Put the flour into a bowl and make a well in the centre. Put in the eggs and salt and one-third of the milk. Mix the egg, salt and milk together with a whisk, then gradually widen the circle to incorporate the flour. Add the rest of the milk and keep whisking until you have a smooth batter. Leave to stand for an hour—it will keep up to 3 days.

2 Make sure your butter is hot and melted and next to the crêpe pan on the stove. Heat the crêpe pan and when it is very hot add a little butter. You need only use enough to prevent the crêpe from sticking—pour off any excess. When the butter begins to brown, pour in 1½ tablespoons of the batter. Tilt the pan in a circular motion to coat the surface thinly and evenly. When bubbles begin to appear, flip the crêpe over with an egg slice and cook until golden brown.

makes about 20

Butternut pancakes

2½ oz/75 g butternut squash
1 egg, separated
1 tablespoon safflower oil
1 cup milk or soymilk
¼ cup apple sauce
1½ cups wholemeal flour
¼ teaspoon sea salt
½ teaspoon cinnamon
1½ teaspoons baking powder

1 Cut the butternut squash into large cubes and steam for 5 minutes until soft, then cool.
2 Beat egg white until stiff. In a separate bowl, beat egg yolk, oil, butternut squash, milk and apple sauce.
3 In another bowl, sift the remaining dry ingredients, then stir in the butternut mixture. Gently fold in the egg white.
4 Lightly oil a large frying pan and heat. Test by sprinkling a few drops of water – if it bubbles the heat is right. For each pancake, pour approximately 3–4 tablespoonfuls of batter into the pan. When bubbles appear on top of the pancakes turn and cook until the other side has just become brown.
5 Serve with real maple syrup and fresh seasonal fruit.

serves 4

Crêpes with ricotta & spinach

Crêpes
1 cup all-purpose (plain) flour
1 tablespoon capsicum juice
1 egg
1 cup milk
pinch salt

Filling
8 oz/250 g spinach
10 oz/300 g ricotta cheese
salt and freshly ground black pepper

1 Beat together the crêpe ingredients and refrigerate for 1½ hour.
2 Stir-fry spinach and add cheese and salt and pepper. Make crêpes then place spinach mixture in crêpes and roll up. If you wish you can sauté sliced mushrooms, add some cream, simmer and pour over crêpes.

serves 4

Hue stuffed pancakes

vegetable oil, for frying
2 oz/60 g all-purpose
  (plain) flour seasoned with
  salt and pepper
2 eggs, beaten
extra vegetable oil, for
  deep frying

Batter
3 oz/90 g rice flour
½ cup coconut milk
3 eggs, beaten
pinch salt

Filling
3 cm piece ginger, peeled,
  chopped
1 clove garlic, chopped
1 tablespoon soy sauce
½ cup white sauce
5 oz/145 g crab meat
3 oz/90 g mushrooms,
  chopped
6 scallions (spring onions),
  chopped
1 oz/30 g bean sprouts
salt and pepper

To serve
lettuce leaves
coriander leaves, chopped
nuoc cham dipping sauce
1 red chilli, seeded and
  finely sliced

1 To make batter, combine rice flour, coconut milk, eggs and salt. Heat some oil in a 8 in/20 cm pan (preferably non-stick), add enough batter to coat base. Cook for 2 minutes. Repeat with remaining batter. Put all pancakes aside.
2 To make filling, blend ginger, garlic, soy and white sauce. Add crab meat, mushrooms, spring onions and bean sprouts and season to taste. Place a spoonful of the mixture on to each pancake. Tuck in ends and roll up so mixture doesn't escape.
3 Carefully roll each pancake in seasoned flour, then in beaten egg. Deep-fry until golden. Serve on lettuce leaves, sprinkled with chopped coriander, accompanied by nuoc cham and sliced chilli.

serves 8

Indian pancakes

3 scallions (spring onions)
1½ cups rice flour
1 teaspoon salt
½ teaspoon baking powder
14 oz/400 ml can coconut milk
2 eggs, lightly beaten
olive oil

1 Trim and finely chop spring onions. Mix rice flour, salt, baking powder and spring onions together. Add half the coconut milk, eggs and whisk until smooth. Whisk in remaining coconut milk.
2 Grease a small frying pan with oil. Spoon about 2 tablespoons of batter into pan. Cook over a medium heat until lightly brown. Turn and cook the other side. Keep warm and serve with curries.

makes 25

Sweetcorn pancakes

¼ cup milk
1 tablespoon melted butter
3½ oz (100 g) canned creamed corn
1 teaspoon dried chopped chives
1 egg
⅓ cup self-rising (self-raising) flour
extra butter for cooking

1 Combine milk, butter, creamed corn, chives and egg in a bowl and season with salt and pepper.
2 Add flour and stir until smooth.
3 Heat a little butter in a fry pan. Pour in quarter of a cup mixture and cook over low heat for about 2 minutes each side or until puffed and golden.
4 Serve pancakes with pan-fried bacon and tomatoes.

Note: These pancakes are great to serve as a snack with cream cheese and ham or smoked salmon.

serves 4

Mussel crêpes

4 lb/2 kg mussels
½ cup dry white wine
2 tablespoons chopped onion
4 parsley stalks, bruised
6 black peppercorns, crushed

3½ oz/100 g all-purpose (plain) flour
2 large eggs
4–6 tablespoons thickened cream
4 tablespoons butter
6 tablespoons fresh parsley, chopped

1 Wash the mussels, discarding any that are open (and do not close when touched). Pull off the beards. Place the wine, onion, parsley stalks and peppercorns in a large pan and bring to a simmer. Add the mussels (in 2 batches) and cover. Cook over high heat for 3–4 minutes shaking occasionally, until they are open.

2 Remove the mussels and discard the shells and any that remain shut. Strain the liquid into a measuring jug and leave to cool. Taste for seasoning. Make the crêpe batter. Place the flour in a bowl or blender and work in the eggs, mussel liquid and 2 tablespoons of cream. (Don't over beat) Allow to stand for 1 hour.

3 Melt 1 tablespoon of butter in a frying pan, swirling it around. Add to the batter and stir thoroughly. To cook crêpes, heat another tablespoon of butter and swirl. Use about 6 oz/175 ml crêpe batter per crêpe. It is easiest to pour from a cup.

4 Lift the pan and pour the batter fast into the middle of the pan and in a circle around, tilting the pan to cover the base. If you overdo the liquid, spoon off anything that doesn't set at once—crêpes should be thin.

5 Return the pan to the heat, shaking it to make sure the crêpe does not stick. Cook for 1 minute until golden underneath, then flip over using a spatula. Briefly cook the other side. Keep warm on a plate while you make more.

6 Warm the remaining cream in a saucepan with the mussel flesh. Spoon the mussels and a little cream onto one edge of a crêpe, sprinkle with parsley and roll up. Serve immediately.

serves 6

Seafood crêpes

12 crêpes (see page 259)
6 scallions (spring onions), finely chopped
2 oz/60 g butter
7 oz/200g canned red salmon, drained and
  flaked
1 egg yolk, lightly beaten
2 teaspoons dry Sherry
4 hard-boiled eggs, chopped
2 teaspoon chives, snipped
½ cup Gruyère cheese, grated

Cream sauce
1½ cups milk
1 bay leaf
½ onion, chopped
5 black peppercorns
2 oz/60 g butter
4 tablespoons plain flour
½ cup cream
salt and white pepper

1 To make the cream sauce, heat the milk slowly in a saucepan over low heat with the
  bay leaf, onion and peppercorns. When bubbles form around the edge, remove from
  the heat, cover and stand for 10 minutes. Meanwhile, melt the butter over low heat,
  stir in the flour and cook, stirring, for 1 minute. Remove from the heat, cool a little,
  then strain in the warm milk and cream. Stir until smoothly blended, then return to the
  heat and stir until boiling. Season with salt and pepper.
2 Preheat oven to 350°F/180°C. Cook the shallots gently in butter until softened. Add
  the salmon and remove from the heat. Fold the egg yolk, sherry, chopped eggs, chives
  and salmon mixture into the cream sauce. Spread in the centre of the crêpes, roll up
  and arrange in one layer in a buttered, ovenproof serving dish. Cover the dish with foil
  and warm for 10 minutes. Uncover and sprinkle with grated cheese. Return to the oven
  and bake uncovered for a further 5 minutes. Serve immediately.

serves 4–6

Flapjacks

1½ cups wholemeal flour
1 cup all-purpose (plain) flour
1 cup rolled oats
½ cup yellow cornmeal
1 tablespoon baking powder
2 teaspoons baking soda (bicarbonate of soda)
½ teaspoon salt
4 oz/125 g frozen unsalted butter, cut into small pieces
4 x 2 oz/60 g eggs
4 cups buttermilk
½ cup honey

1 In a food processor, process the dry ingredients until well blended. Add the butter and process for a further minute or so until the mixture resembles coarse breadcrumbs.
2 Beat the eggs and buttermilk together in a large mixing bowl and stir in the honey. Fold in the flour mixture, until just blended. Heat a heavy frying pan or griddle with a little butter. Ladle the batter on to make 4–5 in/10–12 cm pancakes. Cook on one side until bubbles appear and the underside is golden, then flip over and cook the other side. Serve piping hot with butter and maple syrup.

serves 2

Apple hotcakes

½ cup long-grain rice
juice of 1 lemon
1 Granny Smith apple, grated
¾ cup milk
4 eggs, separated
1 cup all-purpose (plain) flour
1 teaspoon baking powder
pinch of salt
8 oz/250 g mascarpone
1 tablespoon ground cinnamon

1 Combine the rice with 1 cup water in a saucepan. Bring to the boil, reduce heat to low, cover and cook for 10 minutes. Remove pan from heat, stir through lemon juice. Stand covered for 10 minutes.
2 Place rice, grated apple, milk and egg yolks in a mixing bowl and stir to combine. Sift the flour, baking powder and salt into a bowl. Add to the rice mixture and fold until just combined.
3 Combine mascarpone and cinnamon and mix well. Set aside.
4 Place egg whites in a clean dry bowl and beat until stiff peaks form. Fold egg whites through batter in two batches with a large metal spoon.
5 Lightly spray a large non-stick frying pan with canola oil and drop 2 tablespoons of batter per hotcake into the pan (don't cook more than 3 per batch). Cook over medium-low heat for 2 minutes, or until hotcakes have golden undersides. Turn and cook on the other side until golden and cooked through.
6 Dust hotcakes with icing sugar and serve with cinnamon mascarpone.

serves 4

Cinnamon pancakes

1 cup self-raising flour
¼ cup caster sugar
2 teaspoons cinnamon sugar
2 eggs, lightly beaten
¾ cup milk
oil cooking spray
strawberries and bananas, to serve
maple syrup
ice cream

1 Sift the flour in a mixing bowl. Add the sugar and cinnamon sugar. Make a well in the middle and add the eggs and milk. Slowly whisk the mixture until smooth.
2 Spray a non-stick frying pan with oil. Heat the frying pan over low to medium heat. Pour in a ¼ cup mixture and cook the pancakes for 2 minutes on each side or until cooked. Repeat with the remaining mixture.
3 Serve the pancakes topped with sliced strawberries and bananas. Drizzle with maple syrup and serve with scoops of ice cream.

makes 8

Coconut pancakes

½ cup all-purpose (plain) flour
1 tablespoon superfine (caster) sugar
2 eggs, lightly beaten
¾ cup milk or coconut milk
oil spray for cooking
1 cup grated palm sugar or brown sugar
1 pandan leaf
1 cup shredded coconut, toasted
1 papaya, diced
ice cream, to serve

1 Combine flour and sugar in a mixing bowl. Add eggs and milk and whisk mixture until
   smooth. Add a little water if too thick.
2 Heat a frying pan. Spray with oil, then add enough mixture to make a thin pancake.
   Cook pancakes for 1–2 minutes on each side.
3 Combine sugar, ½ cup of water and pandan leaf in a saucepan. Bring to the boil and
   simmer over low heat, stirring until sugar dissolves and syrup thickens slightly.
4 Place coconut and papaya on each pancake and roll up. Serve pancakes with ice cream
   and drizzle with syrup.

makes 8

Maize pancakes with honey

¾ cup self-rising (self-raising) flour
¼ cup fine ground polenta or cornmeal
¼ cup superfine (caster) sugar
2 eggs, lightly beaten
¾ cup buttermilk
oil cooking spray
½ cup warm honey
strawberries and bananas, to serve

1 Sift flour into a mixing bowl. Add ground polenta and sugar. Make a well in the middle
  and stir in eggs and buttermilk. Gradually whisk together until mixture is smooth.
2 Heat a non-stick frying pan over low heat and spray with oil. Spoon ¼ cup mixture into
  pan and cook for about 2 minutes each side or until cooked. Repeat with remaining
  mixture.
3 Serve pancakes with warm honey, sliced strawberries and bananas.

makes 8

Crêpe suzette

1 quantity of crêpe batter (see page 259)
4 lumps cube sugar
3½ oz/100 g butter
juice of 1 orange
few drops lemon juice
½ cup orange-flavoured liqueur or brandy

1 Make the crêpes and stack flat, one on top of the other on a hot dish until all are made.
2 Rub the cube sugar over the rind of an orange until they are well soaked with the aromatic oils. Crush with a fork in a small bowl adding half of the butter.
3 Mix until creamy. Place the remaining butter in a chafing dish or frying pan and add orange juice, lemon juice and liqueur. Bring to the boil and stir in creamed butter and sugar. Place the crêpes in this sauce and coat liberally, as you work, fold the crêpes in quarters.

serves 4

Pikelets

1 cup self-rising (self-raising) flour
pinch of salt
2 tablespoons sugar
1 egg
1 cup milk
2 tablespoons butter
1 teaspoon golden syrup
a little oil or butter for greasing

1 Sift the flour and salt into a bowl and add the sugar. Beat the egg and milk together
   and stir into the flour. Melt the butter and golden syrup together and stir over a low
   heat until melted, then add to the mixture.
2 Grease a griddle or shallow-frying pan with a little oil or butter and when it is hot, drop
   in the batter in spoonfuls (about a tablespoon), a little apart. Cook over a medium heat
   until the underside is browned and small bubbles appear on the surface, then turn and
   brown the other side. Serve warm with butter or cold with jam and whipped cream.

makes about 20

Banana pancakes

Wholemeal pancakes
1 cup wholemeal flour
1¼ cups milk
1 egg
2 tablespoons honey
1 teaspoon oil

Banana topping
2 tablespoons chopped raisins
2 tablespoons honey
squeeze of lemon juice
2 bananas, sliced

Strawberry sauce
8 oz/250 g strawberries, puréed with 2 teaspoons lemon juice

1 To make the pancakes, combine flour, milk, egg, honey and oil in a food processor. Process. Stand for 30 minutes.
2 To make the topping, soak raisins in 3 tablespoons of hot water for 15 minutes. Stir in honey and lemon juice. Pour over bananas and toss.
3 Heat a greased crepe pan over a medium heat. Pour in 3 tablespoons batter. Cook for 1 minute each side or until golden. Keep warm while making remaining pancakes. Place a little topping on each pancake. Fold over and serve with sauce.

serves 6

Caramelised banana pancakes

1 large egg
3½ oz/100g plain flour, sifted
pinch salt
1 cup milk
2 tablespoons butter, melted
sunflower oil
2 large, firm bananas, sliced
3 tablespoons Madeira or dessert wine, or 2 tablespoons Drambuie
2–3 teaspoons demerara sugar

1 Beat the egg, flour, salt and a little milk to a smooth paste. Gradually mix in the remaining milk, then stir in the melted butter.
2 Brush a non-stick, medium-sized frying pan with the oil and heat until very hot. Pour in 2–3 tablespoons of batter, swirling to cover the base of the pan. Cook the pancakes for 1–2 minutes on each side, until golden. Repeat to make 7 more, keeping the pancakes warm and layering them between sheets of baking paper to stop them sticking.
3 Preheat the grill to high. Wipe the pan, add the bananas and Madeira, wine or Drambuie and heat through gently, stirring.
4 When most of the liquid has evaporated, place a spoonful of the banana mixture on each pancake, fold it into quarters and place in a flameproof dish. Sprinkle with the sugar and grill until the tops of the pancakes are golden and lightly caramelised.

serves 4

Orange curaçao pancakes

Batter mixture
1 cup all-purpose (plain) flour
¼ teaspoon salt
2 medium eggs
2 tablespoons melted butter
⅔ cup cold milk
3 tablespoons orange curaçao

Filling
4 large oranges, peeled and diced
¼ cup Cognac
1 tablespoon superfine (caster) sugar
whipped sweetened cream to serve

1 Make batter for pancakes by sifting the flour and salt into a bowl. Make a well in the centre and beat in the combined eggs and ⅔ cup of cold water. Whisk well together then add the milk, orange curaçao and melted butter. Allow to stand in the refrigerator for 1 hour before use.
2 Make the 12 pancakes in the usual way, stack and keep warm. Put the filling ingredients into a frying pan and gently heat through but do not boil.
3 To serve, pile 4 pancakes on each individual plate and top with orange and whipped cream.

serves 4

Drinks

Cappuccino

5½ fl oz/160 ml cup
⅓ espresso (1 shot)
⅓ steamed milk
⅓ milk froth

1 Firmly tamp 1 tablespoon of ground coffee.
2 The pour/extraction should take about 15–20 seconds and should be about ⅓ of the cup.
3 Add ⅓ fresh hot milk.
4 Add ⅓ milk froth, which can sit higher than the rim of the cup.
5 Garnish with a sprinkle of chocolate powder.
6 Serve in a cup or glass.

serves 1

Caffè latte

5½ fl oz/160 ml cup
⅓ espresso (1 shot)
⅔ steamed milk
4 in/10 cm milk froth

1 Firmly tamp 1 tablespoon of ground coffee.
2 The pour should be ⅓ of the glass.
3 Add ⅔ fresh milk that is hot enough to drink almost immediately rather than waiting for it to cool.
4 Scoop milk froth to the top of the glass.
5 Serve in a cup or glass.

serves 1

Hot chocolate

9 fl oz/250 ml cup
1 tablespoon drinking chocolate
9 fl oz/250ml hot milk

1 Mix 1 tablespoon drinking chocolate in a mug with a little hot water or milk to make a smooth, thick liquid.
2 Fill mug with hot frothed milk and sprinkle with chocolate. Serve with marshmallow if desired.

Italian Hot Chocolate
1 Mix ¼ cup unsweetened cocoa, 3 tablespoons sugar and ½ teaspoon arrowroot together until thoroughly blended.
2 Add ¼ cup milk to a medium saucepan and set over low heat. Whisk in the cocoa mixture until thoroughly incorporated and no lumps remain. Add the rest of the milk.
3 Cook, stirring constantly, over medium-low heat, until the mixture is thickened, about 10 minutes.
4 Once the cocoa has thickened, stir in a hint of additional flavourings before serving—⅛ teaspoon vanilla or almond extract or a teaspoon of Grand Marnier would be nice. Dust with cinnamon or nutmeg.

Note: Alternatively, you can substitute half the liquid with coffee to make a nice mocha.

serves 1

Chai latte

¾ cup water
1 stick of cinnamon
4 cardamom pods
4 whole cloves
¼ in/½ cm fresh ginger root (thinly sliced)
3 teaspoons sugar
1½ teaspoons black tea leaves
⅓ cup fresh milk

1 Place water, cinnamon, cardamom pods, whole cloves, and fresh ginger root (thinly sliced) in a pot and bring to the boil.
2 Cover, lower heat and simmer for 10 minutes.
3 Add sugar and again bring to simmer.
4 Next, add tea leaves, remove from heat and cover.
5 Let steep for 3 minutes, then strain.
6 Add fresh milk that is hot enough to drink almost immediately rather than waiting for it to cool.
7 Scoop milk froth to the top of the glass.

serves 1

Bergamot earl grey spicy tea

1 Earl Grey tea bag
2 bergamot leaves
1 cinnamon stick
cinnamon powder
2 fresh lemon slice
honey to taste

1 Pour 1 cup of boiling water over Ceylon tea bag and 2 bergamot leaves, 1 cinnamon
   stick and 1 lemon slice. Remove the tea bag after 10–15 seconds. Stand for 5 minutes
   and stir frequently with the cinnamon stick. Strain, pour into a pretty mug, and add a
   sprinkling of cinnamon powder, a fresh lemon slice and a touch of honey.

serves 1

Classic chamomile tea

¼ cup of fresh or less of dried chamomile flowers
thumb-length sprig of lemon balm
3 allspice berries, lightly cracked
a little honey

1 Cover chamomile flowers with 1 cup of boiling water. Add lemon balm and allspice berries. Stand for 5 minutes. Strain. Add honey to sweeten and stir well. Sip slowly and feel the tension melt away.

serves 1

Rooibos tea

1 teaspoon or 1 tea bag of rooibos
1 slice of fresh lemon and a good squeeze of lemon juice
3 thin slices of fresh ginger
3 cloves
2 sprigs of lemon balm leaves or a thumb-length sprig of spearmint

1 Take rooibos, fresh lemon and lemon juice, fresh ginger, cloves and lemon balm or spearmint.
2 Pour 2 cups of boiling water over everything, stand for 5 minutes, strain.
3 Sweeten with a touch of honey.

serves 1

Banana smoothie

4 fl oz/120 ml milk
½ banana
juice of 1 orange
3–4 drops lemon juice
4 fl oz/120 ml natural (plain) yoghurt
2 teaspoons apple juice concentrate
slice of orange, to garnish

1 Place all ingredients except orange slice in blender with four ice cubes and blend until smooth.
2 Pour into chilled glass and serve topped with a slice of orange and a straw.

serves 1

Berry banana smoothie

6 frozen strawberries
10–12 blueberries
4 fl oz/120 ml milk
1 banana
1 teaspoon honey
2 drops vanilla extract
vanilla sugar

1 Reserve one strawberry and a few blueberries.
2 Place all remaining ingredients except sugar in blender with four ice cubes and blend until smooth.
3 Pour into chilled glass and serve topped with reserved strawberry and blueberries, and a sprinkle of vanilla sugar.

serves 1

Shirley Temple

½ fl oz/15 ml grenadine
8½ fl oz/270 ml ginger ale or lemonade
slice of orange

1 Build over ice. Garnish with the slice of orange.

Note: For a tangy variation to this drink, try a Shirley Temple No.2. Use 2 fl oz (60 ml)
    pineapple juice to a glass half-full of ice. Top with lemonade, float ½ fl oz (15 ml)
    passionfruit pulp on top and garnish with a pineapple wedge and cherry.

serves 1

Index

Published in 2014 by
New Holland Publishers
London • Sydney • Cape Town • Auckland

The Chandlery Unit 114 50 Westminster Bridge Road London SE1 7QY
1/66 Gibbes Street Chatswood NSW 2067 Australia
Wembley Square First Floor Solan Road Gardens Cape Town 8001 South Africa
218 Lake Road Northcote Auckland New Zealand

www.newhollandpublishers.com

A catalogue record of this book is available at the British Library and the National Library of Australia.

ISBN: 9781742575032

Publisher: Fiona Schultz
Design: Lorena Susak
Production Director: Olga Dementiev
Printer: Toppan Leefung Printing Ltd (China)

10 9 8 7 6 5 4 3 2 1

Texture and images p12, 52, 54, and 68: Shutterstock
Images p4 and 10: iStock

Follow New Holland Publishers on
Facebook: www.facebook.com/NewHollandPublishers